they can't hide us anymore

they can't hide us anymore

RICHIE HAVENS

WITH STEVE DAVIDOWITZ

Foreword by James Earl Jones

SPIKE

AN AVON BOOK

AVON BOOKS, INC.
1350 Avenue of the Americas
New York, New York 10019

Library of Congress Cataloging in Publication Data:

Havens, Richie.
They can't hide us anymore / Richie Havens with
Steve Davidowitz ;
foreword by James Earl Jones.
p. cm.
"An Avon book."
Includes index.
1. Havens, Richie. 2. Afro-American singers—United States—
Biography. I. Davidowitz, Steve. II. Title.
ML420.H235A3 1999   99-25889
782.42164'092—dc21   CIP

First Spike Printing: July 1999

SPIKE TRADEMARK REG. U.S. PAT. OFF. AND IN OTHER COUNTRIES, MARCA
REGISTRADA, HECHO EN U.S.A.

Printed in the U.S.A.

FIRST EDITION

QPM   10 9 8 7 6 5 4 3 2 1

www.spikebooks.com

contents

Foreword
by James Earl Jones
ix

Introduction
by Richie Havens
xiii

CHAPTER 1
August 15, 1969
1

CHAPTER 2
Bedford-Stuyvesant, Brooklyn
4

CHAPTER 3
It Takes *More* Than a Village
15

CHAPTER 4
Greenwich Village, U.S.A.
26

v

CONTENTS

CHAPTER 5
Wha? Wha? What Did They Say?
31

CHAPTER 6
Catching 1,000 Rising Stars
50

CHAPTER 7
From Portraits to Songs
58

CHAPTER 8
Live in New York City
66

CHAPTER 9
The Man Who Changed My Life
73

CHAPTER 10
Turning Pro
78

CHAPTER 11
Show Business Disease
93

CHAPTER 12
Mixed Bag
108

CHAPTER 13
Like a Small Earthquake
118

CHAPTER 14
To Make and Interpret Songs
134

CONTENTS

CHAPTER 15
Stormy Forest
151

CHAPTER 16
"The Clock on the Wall"
164

CHAPTER 17
Meeting Michael Sandlofer
173

CHAPTER 18
What Does *Extinct* Mean, Daddy?
186

CHAPTER 19
Getting a *"Great Blind Degree"*
202

CHAPTER 20
From the Twentieth Floor to *Common Ground*
221

CHAPTER 21
Miracles in the Middle East
235

CHAPTER 22
The *Aliens* Among Us
253

CHAPTER 23
The Truth About Drugs
264

CHAPTER 24
Back to the Future
274

CONTENTS

CHAPTER 25
They Really Can't Hide Us Anymore
291

Acknowledgments
303

Discography
307

A Parting Word from Steve Davidowitz
325

Index
327

foreword

I met Richie Havens in 1966 when he and I appeared together, with Moses Gunn, in an off-off-Broadway production at the 73rd Street Theater in Manhattan. Richie was singing and Moses and I were acting in *Bohickee Creek,* a quartet of connected one-act plays built around the lives of Americans in the South in the early 1950s.

Back then, we were just doing what we loved to do, working hard at it, taking chances, trusting a future we couldn't see. Richie had already made a name for himself doing "coffeehouse gigs" in Greenwich Village. Three years later, in 1969, Woodstock catapulted Richie into international view.

"We were living through the early stages of a musical revolution," Richie writes of his early days. It was a revolution he himself has helped to lead and shape. For Richie, music has always been a compass and a passport. Music is also a lifeline for him, a vital connection to the world he lives in and to the people he cares about, which translates to all people. When he was a teenager in Bedford-Stuyvesant in Brooklyn, New York, music even became a literal and symbolic survival mechanism. Richie actually turned his music into safety insurance against the threats of neighborhood gangs. He discovered that even the tough guys liked to sing rock 'n' roll. In a unique act of self-preservation, Richie helped rival gangs work on their vocal harmonies.

That act foreshadowed all that has come later. Through his extraordinary music, Richie Havens has worked to help people around the world find the harmony. Now he is weaving stories as well as songs.

Stepping into this book is like stepping into the room where Richie is performing live, in concert. Richie tells stories like he sings and plays the guitar—straight from the soul.

Music was born in him, but he had to teach himself the techniques to let it loose in the world. He was a painter first. Greenwich Village was his gallery, the street was his studio, ordinary people were his subjects—more than four thousand of them, Richie estimates, over a two-year stint as a street artist. Painting on the street brought him face-to-face with people. He learned how to communicate despite the roadblocks different languages and cultures throw in the way.

Richie has always been able to read people with the eyes of the visual artist, seeing way past the surface into the soul. His painting made him a seer, and his music made him a listener. One reason his fans like to hear him caress that guitar and sing is because he hears *us,* hears what we are hungry for, or worried about, or celebrating, often before we hear it ourselves.

He was educated, as he says, in "Greenwich Village University," but as a painter, a guitarist, a singer, and a composer, Richie is self-taught. He is an American original, self-made, unorthodox, the best kind of rebel who can break old barriers with affection and respect, all the while taking risks. Richie has the courage to open up new territory without a road map.

As his fans know, Richie is continually growing as an artist. Yet for all he has achieved, he is, to his credit as an artist and a human being, still a work in progress.

Perhaps because Richie himself is one of a kind, his work is rooted in respect for my individuality, and yours. At the same time, he believes, as he writes in this absorbing book, that the people of the world are alike in many important ways. This faith in the potential of the great human family permeates his music.

Yes, you are drawn into this book as you are drawn into a Richie Havens concert—comfortable, yet with an edge of excitement; anticipating the familiar, but knowing you'll also be surprised. Richie ranges over a wide spectrum. He'll tell you about life on the streets of Bedford-Stuyvesant, and in the smoky clubs of Greenwich Village. He'll reflect on what Woodstock meant. He'll tell you about his "open-tuning-bar-chord-method" of playing the guitar. He'll tell you about how and why he writes a song.

He'll tell you about people he's met all over the world. He'll talk about the cosmos, and politics, and the entertainment industry, and Autism, and folk music, and our children's future.

Through it all, Richie tells true stories, paints real faces, makes real music, believes, he tell us, in "singing and writing about real emotions, feelings and events." He gives us reality, and he also believes in possibility, in dreams. But when Richie writes that he is seeking to live out the American Dream, he is not talking about money.

As his book reveals, Richie is still marching in the front ranks of a musical revolution, headed for the twenty-first century, with so much left to say.

He writes, "If you do something long enough with passion you will do it well." For most of his life, Richie Havens has been playing and writing and singing with passion and belief. He does it unforgettably well.

This book will help you understand how, and, more important, why.

—JAMES EARL JONES

introduction

This is not really an autobiographical book.

It's a book about the things I have seen and the extraordinary people I met growing up in the Bedford-Stuyvesant section of Brooklyn in the 1950s and Greenwich Village in the 1960s, when it was the center of the music universe. And it is about the Woodstock Festival and the lessons I have learned from people in many places while traveling the world every weekend for more than thirty years.

But this book is not just my story. It's lots of stories about other people—people who became famous, people living ordinary lives, and people who should have been known better than they were. It's about a few special places on this planet that have affected my life and how I live it—about my experiences in several foreign countries and the United States of America as we know it and what it is becoming.

This also is about the common threads of life that I have found from one end of the globe to the other. It is about humorous, talented, and incompetent people who occupy the entertainment industry. And it is about things nobody seems willing say about drug use, why our educational system is failing our youth, and why our children are growing up so fast. It's about modern science and religious philosophy and astrology too. It is about all of these things simply because I have met and worked with some of the most astute people in so many fields and have hungered for firsthand knowledge about everything since I was in my crib.

I was born of a West Indian mother with British roots and a Native American father whose own father came East with Buffalo Bill's Wild West Show. I started out being called a folksinger by many, or as the man who was the first onstage at the Woodstock Music and Arts Fair, both of which I am proud to be, even though my music continues to evolve as I do. In fact, I feel like I have lived more than one life in my time on this planet and will be living a few more: some quite simple, some using every manner of modern device, including a few I invented myself.

I have written this book because I love sharing stories about the way things seem and how they may be changed or accepted. Communication is why I sing, why I draw and paint, and why I live and breathe. I am a work in progress and this book is both an act of communication about what has passed in front of my eyes and a step beyond the past toward a new direction.

This is not my autobiography: *This is what I am doing.*

—RICHIE HAVENS

they can't hide us anymore

CHAPTER

august 15, 1969

I was in New York City and I could feel the swell of energy 100 miles away. Nobody seemed to care that the Woodstock Festival was no longer going to take place anywhere near Woodstock. The only thing that mattered was that it was going to happen. Today.

I left the city at five-thirty in the morning on the day I was supposed to play—the first day—and drove straight to the Howard Johnson Hotel in White Lake, New York, without a hitch. We were only a few miles away from the farm and all the bands had been told to come there first.

I was lucky to get up the road so smoothly. By seven-thirty in the morning, I was sitting in the lobby with my band. I wasn't worried. I was fifth in the order and wasn't scheduled to go on for hours. But at two in the afternoon, I was half-asleep when news came that there was no music; still no way to get through.

RICHIE HAVENS

From the edge of the hotel parking lot I could see traffic stopped cold on the approach road. I could tell right there that the crowd was much larger than anyone was saying.

The road to the stage had disappeared. It was now a wall-to-wall parking lot of abandoned cars. The main highways were backed up with traffic that wasn't going anywhere. The Northbound Quickway (Route 17) had just been closed by the state police . . . The whole thing was beginning to look pretty shaky.

Michael Lang, one of the promoters, rushed back and forth nervously on a motorcycle, weaving between the crowds, riding up and down the hills trying to figure out ways to get a few musicians to the stage. He was mumbling to himself and sweating and we were beginning to think we were all stuck. Right there. No music. At all.

Yet somehow, through all sorts of missed connections and broken leads, Michael managed to find someone with a glass bubble helicopter about twenty miles away. Now here it was, dropping slowly into the parking lot right outside my hotel window. The prop blades made the air sound like shotguns going off. This would be my first helicopter ride and my first good look at what was really happening here.

We were squeezed into the glass bubble cockpit. We were the perfect choice; there were only three of us and we had the fewest instruments. Me; my guitarist, Deano (Paul Williams); and my drummer, Daniel Ben Zebulon. We were sitting behind the pilot with two conga drums, two guitars squeezed between us. The glass surrounded us, top to bottom.

Looking below my feet, I could see the ground clearly, as

if I was sitting on air. I got dizzy for a second. It felt like I was riding a *stem* that was holding two seats. And we were moving 100 miles an hour.

It was beautiful below me. A sea of trees—the tops of them whizzing beneath me in the wash of the helicopter's props. So much green; gray shades of leaves flipped upside down; slight hints of orange and red, the first hues of autumn.

We banked a bit to the left and the sea of trees changed into a different kind of sea, just as beautiful. My mouth dropped when I saw all those people, hundreds of thousands of them. Definitely more than the 250,000 reported in the New York papers the following morning, a whole lot more like half a million on the first day.

It was awesome, like double Times Square on New Year's Eve in perfect daylight with no walls or buildings to hold people in place. The people filled the field and formed a human blanket across the road to the other side of the hill and into the forests all around the field, where nobody could possibly see the stage.

Hovering above the hill, looking all around, my eyes could not take it all in, but I knew what to call it.

"We finally made it," I told myself. *We've all finally made it above ground. They won't be able to hide this picture from the rest of the country.*

I had come to Woodstock with a feeling that I was not one of few, but one of many and the moment we touched ground I knew that was true. My thoughts drifted back to people I grew up with, people I wished could be there too.

bedford-stuyvesant, brooklyn

W e always had music and art in my house, probably because of the neat mix in our blood. My mom's parents came from the British colonies in the Caribbean; my father's father was a Blackfoot Native American from Montana who traveled the country with Buffalo Bill Cody and his Wild West Show. He and his brother spent some time on the Shinnecock Indian Reservation on Long Island, where he met his wife and moved to Brooklyn. My father was the youngest of five and at nineteen he met and married my mother, who was twenty. I was their first child.

My father was a hard worker who made Formica tables. He was a pretty good musician too, a piano player with a feel for jazz. There were six kids and my grandmother was right there helping out my mom, a skilled bookbinder who also worked.

We lived side by side with Irish, German, French, Italian, Greek, Jewish, and Czechoslovakian people. The list could go

My 8th grade graduating class. That's me on the second row left.

on and on. It was post-World War II, a brand-new world. Most of my friends and schoolmates were firstborn Americans and it was easy for us to do things together. As kids we saw few real differences. There were Irish policemen and Jewish tailors and Italian grocers and shoemakers; there were Polish bakers and Chinese laundries and just about every ethnic and religious group you could imagine. We were each other's neighbors and customers.

People trusted each other. Families would not have survived if the corner grocer didn't trust Mrs. Jones or Mr. Dombrowksi to "pay next week." And the same for the "coal man" who delivered fuel to the furnaces of Bed-Stuy to keep three-generation families warm through the bitter cold winters. Our streets were clean and safe and few of us felt the sting of racial prejudice in our daily lives. There was opportunity if you wanted it.

My father worked days and my mother worked nights until I was nineteen, so my grandmother, Beatrice Elizabeth Gay, was responsible for my manners and morality. She was a strong-willed, beautiful woman who was born in the British Isles and she had a love for music of all kinds. She broadened my musical appreciation at every opportunity, teaching me Jewish folk songs and Irish ballads and playing old recordings of Caribbean island music she had carried with her from Barbados. She also was very religious. Every Sunday she would gather the family together. They would kneel at her bed while she prayed for everyone she could think of, from those in hospitals to those who had no homes or food and everyone in between. Before they went to church, I was the baby on the bed.

During World War II, when I was too young to go to school, I would stay with her through most of the day while my parents worked. My grandmother lived in an apartment in the Brooklyn community of Brownsville at the time. There were always people knocking on her door, out of work or hungry, and she would feed them and make sure they left her house clean.

Until things got better, her house was open to anyone. We went to church every Sunday and she never failed to teach us prayers for the hungry and needy in this world . . . And she was a legend in Brooklyn for her fabulous wedding cakes.

They were rum fruitcakes that took weeks to put together. I sometimes watched her in awe on the final day when she would decorate them, using all kinds of different tools and trimmings. She was an artist. And she made enough cakes to help my grandfather, who was a longshoreman, buy a house in 1937. The whole family lived in that house until one by one her children married. We weren't rich, but no one else who owned a home in Brooklyn was either. It took a lot of hard work to get the money together to buy a house and a lot more hard work to pay the mortgage. My grandmother, being a housewife, cleaned homes and made her wedding cakes to save enough to buy a three-story building on Macon Street in Brooklyn and later—in the 1950s—the house on Howard Avenue a few blocks away.

My grandmother knew I was different and I knew it too. I knew most of the people around me didn't have any *real* answers about life, or what was happening in our fast-changing world. We were all guessing; nobody really knew why we were born, why we were here, what we were supposed to be doing, or where we were going. Life was day to day.

Jackie Robinson had been with the Brooklyn Dodgers for almost ten years when things started crumbling in Bed-Stuy. Don Newcombe and Roy Campanella and Sandy Amoros were

A 1998 visit to my Howard Avenue building—now restored back to its original beautiful condition. (*Photo by Steve Davidowitz*)

Dodgers and nobody really saw them as black pioneers anymore.

They were our Brooklyn Bums, the same as Gil Hodges, Pee Wee Reese, or Carl Furillo. But in the mid-1950s big changes started happening all around us. Suddenly Bed-Stuy seemed to become black and Puerto Rican. Suddenly there were street gangs and drugs and major breakdowns taking place in every corner of the community.

It all happened because of a domino effect that no one knew how to stop. First the population in Bed-Stuy began to explode. As more people moved in, we all thought there would be more jobs, more businesses, more people doing good things. But it didn't work out that way. Most of the people who came had very few skills and they didn't have much money or education.

Overcrowding pushed safety nets and social services to the breaking point and drove a lot of good families and businesses away. Why should they stick around when they were losing money, or being robbed in their own stores or on their own front steps? We didn't know how it was anywhere else, but our community wasn't integrated anymore. It was *disintegrating*. I think I was very lucky to grow up in a family that stayed together through all the tough times. Not many in my neighborhood did.

There were half-empty buildings that needed repair, cardboard-covered windows, broken glass in school yards, mean graffiti on subway walls, swastikas on sidewalks in front of the last Jewish deli, drunks sleeping it off under stairwells, kids shooting dice and passing joints between them, cussin' and rankin' each other out, acting tough.

The whole depressing scene seemed to feed on itself and brought about a lot of resentment and racism I had never seen before. The truth is that I never experienced racism while I was growing up. I may have been naïve, but before I was a teenager, I didn't even have any consciousness of slavery. In my mind, slaves had been freed a long time ago by Abraham Lincoln. It was a terrible irony for me to learn that the racism running wild in my own neighborhood was being brought on by those who feared the mass exodus from the South by blacks whose only crime was seeking escape from the brutality of vicious racism down there.

The irony goes even deeper than that, as some of us came to understand later on.

In the mid-1950s the South was a worthy target for the newly born civil rights movement, with the Klan and all the separate-but-hardly-equal drinking fountains, bathrooms, schools, and school buses. But the movement came years too late for many Southern black families and it raised the stakes for the narrow-minded whites who were clinging to control.

Black people in the South were fired for no reason, or they were publicly humiliated. There were roadside killings and churches burned and daughters raped in the woods.

And what of justice? Where were the local, state, and national authorities who had pledged to uphold the Constitution? And the "free press"? Where were the great journalists to expose the Klan or other anti-American groups? It became clear to me as a very young person that the "America" they talked about in school did not really exist yet.

Almost half a century later, looking back on what was going on down there, I think it was a disgrace almost as bad as what happened in Germany. So many people looked the other way and we're still paying for that—all of us.

A lot of black families moved as fast as they could out of the South; they moved out of Alabama and Georgia and Mississippi and the Carolinas and headed north, joining cousins and distant friends in Washington, D.C.; Philadelphia; Detroit; the Bronx; and my neighborhood too.

Those of us born in Brooklyn didn't know what was really happening.

By the time I was sixteen, things were so bad in Bed-Stuy that our schools began to feel like detention centers. Most teachers got real good at taking attendance and herding us off to assembly or gym. They never had trouble giving homework assignments and passing out grades without really going over things. There really wasn't much teaching going on—or learning, for that matter. Sitting at lunch waiting for my friends one day, it hit me that I had not learned one thing I really wanted to know about, so six months before graduation, I quit. My family needed what I could contribute and I needed to know more. A lot more. About everything.

I listened to my senses; tried to learn how to communicate; asked myself questions about what was really going on around me and why people do the things they do. And when I left school, all I really wanted was to soak up as much as I could.

By the time my original high school class graduated, I was certain I had a better all-around education outside the school system than I could have gotten sticking around. I learned what I wanted to. The library became my schoolhouse and the books my teachers. I was interested in things we lacked as a society. I consciously worked hard to understand what was going on and where I fit in the world around me.

I probably worked and quit twenty different jobs between the time I was sixteen and eighteen—not because I couldn't do them, but because I did them well enough to get bored and had to move on.

For the next four years, I went to libraries and read all the books I could find on astronomy and the cosmos. I loved science, especially books about the planet Earth and space travel, and books that talked about the human mind. In fact, two of the first books I took out were almost unreadable to me, but I plodded through them, reading about multiple personalities in a volume by Sigmund Freud and about astrological psychology in an equally intense book by Carl Jung.

I believed then, as I do now, that my calling in life has always been to study the human mind, to be my own "mental surgeon." I thought every problem mankind ever had lived inside the mind. The whole subject really fascinated me. Still does. I even remember when my grandmother asked me, "What do you want to be when you grow up?" I was six years old and said with no hesitation, "I want to be a brain doctor."

"A *brain doctor?*" she asked. "Yes," I told her. "I think what makes people sick is in their brains and if I could cut the sickness out, they would be all right."

Even at that early age, I loved to sing and so did many of my friends. I sang in the church choir and when I sang for an audition on a radio show, everybody in the neighborhood seemed to take pride in that. The music that our parents listened to was coming from dance bands and traditional pop songs and movie scores: the music of Frank Sinatra, Vic Damone, Billy Eckstine, Nat "King" Cole, and others from the big band era. But rock 'n' roll was coming to life; it was the language to be learned in the neighborhood.

I remember my father explaining to me how the movie business was becoming the driving force behind the expansion of the recording business. This was the early 1950s and every other film was a musical—or so it seemed. People left the theaters humming and singing the songs they heard on the big screen. The record companies catered to the demand, but the changing times and the economy made it difficult for big bands to stay together or travel. So they grew smaller until they reached "combo" size, the smallest number of instruments needed to get the same songs across. It was these small dance bands, or combos, that led to the development of early rock 'n' roll records like "Rock Around the Clock." This was still dance music. But on the far end of the radio dial—the so-called other side of the fence—was rhythm and blues, which featured single African American performers and groups of men and women singing beautiful ballads in four-part harmony—like the Spaniels, the Harptones, the Diablos. This was different for the black community and their children . . . us.

In these doo-wop groups we began to hear music that also appealed to our parents, but it wasn't until Frankie Lymon and the Teenagers became a household name ("Why Do Fools Fall in Love") that every kid on the block felt as though they could do the same thing. It was all so easy, so accessible, and the effect was dramatic, even though no one really could see exactly what was taking place. Rock 'n' roll was merging with rhythm and blues and the new form was becoming the newsletter of the young, our own classroom in which we would learn many things they weren't teaching us in our schools or in our homes.

it takes *more* than a village

O n the streets, there was another kind of education you had to have to survive.

Some kids I knew were killed by street gangs and the police. Some of my closest friends were badly beaten up by cops, who didn't seem to care that you were not part of a gang or trying to stay free of drugs. If you were on the street at the wrong time, or seen walking around the block with somebody they hassled before, you were sure to get hassled, or busted, or worse, beat up for nothing.

I can't tell you how many times I felt like I was on a different planet—or wished I had been. Or how many people were beaten down by all the hard changes, except it was more people than I can count, people who were suddenly out of work when the businesses started to close and the Italians and Jews and Polish families moved away. Suddenly the daily struggle to bring home food and to keep a family together was breaking more families apart. I can't tell you how many young people began to turn to drugs to escape the pain of failure in their lives, but I can tell you about one: a very close friend, Kenny Schneider.

Kenny was German, lived in the Bushwick section on the other side of Broadway, "across the tracks" where it had always been mostly white. Families still owned homes in Bushwick—real houses, not apartments—and there were trees and gardens there, although Kenny's family lived in a rented flat.

Kenny sang the hell out of the first tenor part in the best doo-wop group I ever put together. I did a lot of that in those days. Many of my friends were hassled by street gangs and sometimes the only way to get from one place to another was to get in with the "right" people. Besides, I loved it. There was nothing I enjoyed more than hearing voices sing in harmony.

The street gangs of the fifties weren't into heavy-duty firepower like the rapid-fire weapons on the streets today. They made their own "Saturday night specials"—.22-caliber pistols put together with metal tubing, a piece of wood, and some tape. Switchblade knives actually were the weapons of choice, brass knuckles and homemade blackjacks too.

Every gang had their areas carved out and their own logo, just like they do now, and in some ways it probably was harder for innocent bystanders to walk from one territory to another. There was dope selling, but not by the street gangs and not anything close to the way today's gangs ruthlessly control drug use like the old Mafia and seek to expand it for major profits. In the late 1950s you didn't find much cocaine on the street.

If there was any, it was in the hands of the older generation. Drinking wine and beer was how most teenagers dealt with their conflicts. There was very little grass or hard stuff, the kind you had to have two or three times a day once you were hooked. But it was creeping in while street gangs were carving out their territories.

I was not a celebrity in Bed-Stuy, but everybody I grew up with knew I was into music and it didn't take much for me to figure out that there were a lot of "tough guys" who liked rock 'n' roll. Some of them had their own doo-wop groups that mingled and competed at various school contests and at the Apollo Theatre in Harlem.

To keep my own life intact and to stay out of the way of the gang scene, my friends who sang with me and I started helping some of the gang members work on harmonies. Pretty soon I was doing it as a regular thing, organizing a group in one section of Bed-Stuy and another group a few blocks away. Sometimes my friends would come with me and be allowed to pass through rival gang territories next time through. The camaraderie of music became our passport. I don't even remember how many different groups or combinations of people I sang with, but it was a lot, maybe a few dozen.

A few times I did go alone to a bar several blocks away from my neighborhood where a fellow named Clarence "Eighty-Eight" Keys played a few nights a week and doubled as an accompanist for those in the audience who wanted to sing a song or two late in the evening. I had no idea that I would eventually become a singer-songwriter, but I went there to sing classic songs that I learned listening to my father play. Songs like "The Masquerade Is Over" and "Summertime." These were my first and only solo singing experiences in Brooklyn.

Singing groups on street corners were pretty big in Bed-Stuy all the way through the fifties. Rock 'n' roll was beginning to break into the mainstream. Music by the Cleftones, the Jive Bombers, the Penguins, the Dells, and the Five Satins was being played on the radio regularly, crossing over from the pure black music stations on the far end of the dial to the mainstream and network stations. We were living through the early stages of a musical revolution and our parents were suddenly wondering if the world had gone mad. It hadn't. It was just waking up.

I taught all the different harmony parts, did all our choreography, and sang baritone in the background. We were good and this got us through any part of Bed-Stuy any time we wanted. Music made it all possible.

One of the groups I put together was pretty special. There were six of us and we were all good friends, five African Americans and Kenny. We were really good. We sang and rehearsed many hours every day and played and won a whole lot of amateur doo-wop singing contests for nearly two years. We were good, as good as anybody on the radio.

Every time we did a public gig, there was always somebody who wanted to sign us up for a record deal or a job in the city. But our bass singer, Claude Doggett—my best friend—just happened to have a father who was a fundamentalist minister and he wouldn't have any of that. He said we were singing "the Devil's music." Funny thing about that was that Claude's uncle was Bill Doggett, the same Bill Doggett who was doing pretty well with "the Devil's music," especially with "Honky Tonk," a funky little instrumental that skyrocketed to number two on the national pop charts.

Anyway, singing was one of Kenny's many talents. He was even a better writer, a poet who had a smooth sense of rhythm even when he was writing straight prose. He had an eye for things and he seemed to know just the right phrase or line to finish off a point. Kenny probably threw away more fine poetry than most published poets. He was fun to be around and we all knew that someday he was going to be one of those people everybody in the world gets to read. Kenny was going to be important.

I liked to write poetry too, so Kenny and I got along great, trading ideas. Guys in the neighborhood called us "beatniks," although neither of us knew what the hell that meant until we read a big Sunday spread in the *Daily News* about the beatniks in Greenwich Village. But something was going wrong with Kenny and I was probably the last in the group to figure out what it was. All I noticed was that he had stopped drinking the beer he always brought for our rehearsals.

Kenny was on drugs, hard drugs. *Heroin.*

I only found out about it when the guys in the group said they couldn't handle hanging out with a junkie. They just stopped trusting him and the next thing I knew we were done and it was just him and me.

I couldn't quit on Kenny as a friend. We had both started to dream the same dream; we both wanted to go to the Village and see the world. We shared the same feelings; we were both poets. We didn't know exactly what kind of artists we were or what we were going to do, but there was just too much there to go our separate ways. Besides, I just knew I could get him off dope if I tried hard enough.

He talked to me. He told me how he was getting his money to pay for his habit. He wasn't stealing, he said. His grandmother, like mine, was trying to help him. Where mine gave me music and kept a strict watch on my values, his gave him fifteen dollars twice a week for doing a few errands. She knew what was going on. She knew Kenny's father was getting hit hard in our local depression and he was taking it out on Kenny in every way possible.

Nothing Kenny did was ever good enough for his father. Not his writing, his work at the Rheingold brewery, where his father also worked, or the thousand and one things he tried to do to win approval. His mother wasn't exactly balancing things out either. I don't think they ever hit him, but they sure beat the hell out of him emotionally—every day.

I heard some of the things they yelled at him. I wouldn't want anybody saying those things to me, calling him a worthless bum and spicing every attack with four-letter words.

"Every day it's like that," he told me. "I just can't take it much longer. I don't sleep, I don't eat, I just try to shut my mind to it as much as I can." And it came out in his poetry.

When I found out about his habit and didn't run away

from him, Kenny started seeking me out in all kinds of situations. When he needed to buy drugs, he would call me and ask me to go with him. He was afraid of being beaten up and robbed, which happened to him more than once and this at least slowed him down enough to seek help. But the minute he came out of a program, he was right back at it. Anyway, I went with him and that seemed to be enough to protect him. But the truth is, I sometimes wanted to kill the bastards, or at least turn them in to the cops, whom we hated just as much.

The truth is, I probably could have busted every drug dealer in Brooklyn. I was the guy who found himself waiting in strange places, hanging in there with Kenny dozens of times. It sickened me, but this was my friend and as long as he was alive, there was hope. I really didn't know a whole lot about heroin, but I could see it was destroying someone who had a lot going for him.

We went to the Village together. We tried out our poetry in front of people for the first time together. We rode the subways all night long many times and I tried to get him to stop taking drugs by making him drink brandy, to get him drunk. How stupid was that! I thought one would be better than the other.

When we did make it to the Village together, I knew I was not going to last very much longer in Brooklyn. Kenny was getting sick more often, going in and out of drug programs, going down a little farther, a little deeper, every day. And a few things happened at almost the same time that practically pushed me on my way.

One afternoon there was a bloody family fight on the street corner and the cops came. When the fight was over, the guy who had his ass kicked was looking to get off on someone else. I recognized him as one of the jerks who sold Kenny drugs. And I think he had seen me with Kenny a few times.

"What're you lookin' at?" he said, pushing me back a step. My reflex was partly out of fear, partly out of what had been building up in me over Kenny and the way my once peaceful neighborhood was turning to crap. I recoiled with a right to his jaw as hard as I could. He literally flew backward over the railing of the brownstone building behind him. I didn't wait around to see his next move. I was gone. I had never hit anyone before in my life. I felt bad about it. And good. He deserved exactly what he got.

A few days later, I was sitting in the Borough Bar on the corner of Broadway and Gates Street when the cops came in to roust half a dozen guys at the bar. I was at the corner table—in the dark—writing like I always did. Nobody usually bothered me; even though I was underage, the cops never seemed to notice me. I only ordered Cokes and began to feel as though I was invisible.

While something happened in this bar almost every weekend, this time there was a knock-down-drag-out fight with chairs and a few broken bottles. Somebody was even tossed into the glass behind the bar, just like the movies. No wonder they called it the "Bucket of Blood." I wasn't too thrilled about going back there to put my blood in with the rest. I had spent a year there unnoticed, drinking Coca-Colas and writing my poetry.

Just about the same time all this was going on, I happened to see a doo-wop group singing in the one safe park left in my neighborhood. They were kids, four of them, including the two younger brothers of Bernice Wise—my girlfriend at the time—the younger brother of Paul Williams, and another of their friends. I had no idea they could sing. The oldest was maybe fourteen, the youngest ten. They were so fantastic I knew I had to do something for them, I just knew I had to take them into the Village with me and blow some people's minds. Their harmony was tight and they wrote their own songs.

On my next trip into the Village, I impulsively borrowed a friend's guitar. I'd never played the guitar before, but somehow I knew I could tune it to a chord and give these kids some music behind their voices. I barely learned three chords and played the guitar flat on my lap, like a dulcimer.

We practiced at my girlfriend's house a couple of weekends and without permission from their parents I took the kids to the Village. We set up in Washington Square Park on the MacDougal Street side near Waverly.

About eighty people surrounded us while they sang about twelve songs. A couple of guys in the crowd took off their hats and passed them around. There was about $150 in the guitar case on the ground and maybe another $80 in the two hats. Those people loved these kids. So did the two guys with the hats. They ran off with the $80. Still, $150 was a hell of a lot of money in 1960 for four kids and by the time we did another set there was $250 more.

They made about $133 apiece and I was able to tell them all the way back to Brooklyn: "See? This is what you guys can be doing. You can make real money, honest money, using your talent." I felt they had to see that. I didn't want to see these kids ending up on drugs or dead.

I heard the message I was giving them in my own head. I knew I was going to the Village soon and never coming back.

My mom was kind of expecting me to leave. She was even hinting that I should. "When are you going to give up the odd jobs you do and get a real job?" she would say to me. "Or maybe you should send some of your poetry or drawings to a magazine."

A couple of weeks later—after I took the kids back to the Village to play on the stage of the Cafe Wha?—I had a conversation with Kenny that told me it was time. He was not going to make it. He was losing a lot of weight.

He looked awful. His voice was cracking and he had the cold sweats. He was sitting on a bench near a bus stop on my side of Broadway. He didn't want me to go with him to buy drugs this time; he just wanted to tell me something.

"Swear to me, Richie, that you'll never use drugs like me."

I didn't need him to say that, and while I could see he was losing it, I had to let him know that he was the best example I could ever have not to do what he was doing.

"Kenny, just look at you," I said. "Why would I want to take drugs? You used to be a hundred and fifty pounds and full of wonderful thoughts. Now you probably don't weigh a hundred and ten. Jeezus, Kenny, you're in constant pain, pain the drugs don't even take away. You're the best reason I will ever need, Kenny."

I loved Kenny and we had many good memories together, but when I strip away all the hurt and the sickness I felt him go through as he slipped away, I knew that his life's gift to me was to make me know for sure that drugs were not the answer. It was something to carry out of Brooklyn, something to never forget.

CHAPTER

greenwich village, u.s.a

4

I wasn't a musician when I came to town. I wasn't anything, but I knew instantly that the Village was home for me. I felt as if I had crossed an ocean or something and finally found the promised land. It was my old neighborhood! Young people from all over the world—going to New York University.

The first day I walked up and down MacDougal and Bleecker streets and around Washington Square Park I knew that I would survive somehow in the Village. Why not? It's what I did in Brooklyn. But I did not start out as a singer. In fact, I had begun to draw portraits while traveling back and forth to Brooklyn after leaving high school and I continued to draw them for more than two years before I performed onstage.

I had always done some light sketching and was fascinated by the dozens of portrait artists doing their thing all along the Village streets. It didn't look so hard. And they were making ten dollars and fifteen dollars a pop for portraits engraved in copper and a lot more for pencil or charcoal. So like a jerk, I said, "I could do that" out loud, and of course the owner of the storefront gallery promptly hired me—almost on a dare.

I was lucky he gave me two pieces of copper, because I actually etched the face of my first customer too big to fit the frame. But the next thing I knew I was sitting in front of his gallery doing all kinds of portraits, mostly in pencil and with etching tools on copper sheets. I had never done charcoal before. It wasn't an easy medium to control, but somehow I got the hang of it on the very first day.

Working three or four days a week for those two years, I must have done more than four thousand portraits and made up to $600 a day for this guy and about $300 a day for myself. That was a ton of money at the time. A *ton* of money. But I gave a lot to friends who needed it and took some back to my mom and my girlfriend's family in Brooklyn while spending plenty just as freely. Actually, it was a rare week when I would have much left at all. That's because my philosophy about money in those days was the same as it is now: If you have a lot of money in your pocket, you're probably blowing it, man. Money is there to be spent. To me the principal object of money is really quite simple: Use it to change what you can. Control your own world. Find a lot of good ways to spend it! Make your own day!

Spend it on family and friends, spend it on the people you love and their futures; spend it on education and on things you believe in—things that will make better art or a better life.

But by all means, spend it. Spend it in order to enjoy what is there to be enjoyed.

In my case, I didn't work to make money. I did portraits to pay my way and to continue my "education" on the streets of Greenwich Village. I worked because I loved what I was doing and who I was meeting. Drawing portraits, I met thousands of people from everywhere. We shared stories about their countries and our families, about where we came from, what we saw and felt. We looked at each other and laughed at each other. We communicated almost instantly across language barriers and cultural backgrounds. In fact, there were so many instances of straight, honest contact that I learned a valuable lesson about people that would be reinforced several years later when I took my first of more than thirty trips out of the country.

The people of the world are so much alike in so many important ways that *all* of our fears about each other are simply based on propaganda and narrow-minded prejudices against different cultures and religions. Usually this is because of what someone else teaches you, not what really is.

That was what I learned as a young man on the Village streets, meeting strangers from everywhere. That was what I found talking with human beings who happened to have yellow, brown, or black skin, or ate different foods, or worshipped God in so many infinitely different ways, or even believed that there was no God at all.

I loved being on the streets of "Greenwich Village Univer-

THEY CAN'T HIDE US ANYMORE

Direct from the sixties. (*Photo by Günter Zint*)

sity." I felt unbelievably lucky to have stumbled upon this precious spot on the planet.

There were hundreds of painters, writers, poets, singers, comedians, and songwriters developing ideas and perfecting their work. There were all-day conversations about new books and experimental plays and there were all-night conversations about what was happening in our lives. Those of us who migrated there and stayed for more than a few days seemed more inclined than the people we left behind to share openly what we thought about things; what we wanted to embrace. We traded songs and poems and political arguments. We had no plan, no road map to follow. We didn't know where we were going, but a lot of us seemed to be looking around, taking stock of things.

We learned not to be afraid; to be ourselves, together. And together we exercised our freedom to say what was really on our minds, never noticing the collective results. We discovered our similarities and this absolutely diminished the differences we had been misled to believe existed.

There was so much talent and energy in the Village of the early 1960s that we instinctively knew that big changes in our American culture were brewing all around us. The air was electric and it was going to be like that for most of the decade.

wha? wha? what did they say?

The very first singer I saw perform in a Greenwich Village club was Noel Stookey, who later would give me a lot of encouragement to perform myself. And not long thereafter, I also saw two other singer-songwriters—Dino Valenti and Fred Neil—doing the kind of songs that would become the foundation of all I believe in today. Yet the very first "star" I saw on a Village stage was a legend who disappeared quickly from view. His name was Victor "Superman" Brady, he was from St. Croix in the Caribbean, and he was making a good living as the featured attraction in the Cafe Wha?

The Cafe Wha? was an early Village club that changed quickly from a poetry-reading coffeehouse during the "beatnik years" of the fifties into a music and comedy club that attracted the tourist trade. Manny Roth, who previously owned a casual Village hangout—the Cock and Bull—bought the Wha? And Victor "Superman" Brady was his big star, the headline performer on a nightly show that usually included a solo performer, a comedian, a musical group, and sometimes a guest performer from outside the Village scene.

Brady had a steel drum band that fit in with the calypso music craze that was enjoying a return to popularity spurred on by Harry Belafonte and limbo-dancing contests. Brady had his act down pat and the tourists who poured in to the Village would line up to see him. He had a good thing going, but in a year or so, Brady was going to be blown out of the water by Bob Dylan; Joan Baez; Odetta; Peter, Paul, and Mary—a huge tidal wave of traditional and contemporary folksingers and songwriters who were ready to raise the consciousness of American music and society at large.

The Wha? was paying Brady about $125 a week, which was about $100 more than they paid anybody else. The limbo dancers, stand-up comics, folk musicians, and poets who played on the bill had to pass the hat and make a sales pitch after each set to make their dough. The speech would go something like: "Ladies and gentlemen, please forgive me for this intrusion. But I have three young daughters at home and a sick wife. So, if you like my music, don't be shy about dropping some of your appreciation into the hat Linda is passing about. And as I sing the next song, a gentle reminder: Certain kinds of money don't make as much noise as others. Thanks again."

Ten dollars for a night's work was pretty good, especially with White Castle burgers costing fifteen cents each and Night Owl fries a quarter. A fifteen-dollar night was three squares and a new set of guitar strings. Nobody challenged the system, not while Brady was the featured performer and the Wha? was completely packed every night.

The Wha? was no minor league deal. Not many clubs in New York were doing as much business as the Wha? or were as skillful milking dollars from their customers. The crowds began pouring in during the afternoon and continued to grow past midnight. There were so many tourists on the streets you couldn't walk in the opposite direction on the sidewalk. Never mind the locals from New Jersey and Long Island. There were foreigners and people from faraway states. Just crossing the street was like running through the Green Bay Packers' defensive line. You had to zig and zag to daylight. The Village was like Mardi Gras every weekend. During the summer, it was like that every day and night.

"No cover, no minimum," the hawkers would say in front of each club, but as soon as you took the bait, you would find out that there was an "admission charge." It was a con game that everybody played.

Another place would say, "No charge for admission . . . no charge for your first drink," but there was a two-drink minimum and the second drink was three bucks and it was coffee, or cola with a trace of rum extract. This at a time when a bottle of beer was thirty-five cents and Pepsi a dime. Another place would promise two free drinks but hit you for their three bucks at the door. No matter what they said, they always got their three dollars. This was showbiz. Everybody in the Village felt they were in showbiz.

The Wha? had it down to a science. When Brady finished his set, a booming baritone voice filled the club from a closet-sized sound booth. The voice sounded like Moses coming down from Mount Sinai. "LADIES AND GENTLEMEN, WOULD YOU PLEASE LEAVE BY THE REAR EXIT . . . PLEASE BE CONSIDERATE OF THOSE WAITING OUTSIDE FOR THE NEXT SHOW, WHICH WILL START IN TWENTY MINUTES." The room would empty out in five minutes flat and the four- or five-act show would begin all over again in ten. Standing room only . . . That's why Brady got the big bucks. Sometimes the performer who shared the stage with him would even hear a voice whisper from offstage. "*Pssst.* Cut it short. We got to get Victor back on." Performers like Richard Pryor, Bill Cosby, Tim Hardin, Fred Neil, and Lou Gossett, Jr., to name just a few, took a backseat to Victor and his steel band.

Victor had something rare for the times. The steel drum was far from the primitive instrument it seemed at first glance. Made by hand from large oil drums left on the shores of the islands that dot the Caribbean, these incredible instruments were flipped over and the bottom was hammered into a con- cave shape. Then, using a punch, small pockets of different sizes were marked out and later were hammered out in reverse, convexly. They were tuned with a steel hammer and played with seven-inch dowel sticks wrapped with rubber bands on one end. They made the most beautiful sounds. And Victor was the Guy.

There were many wonderful talents in the Village who are barely remembered and plenty who deserve to live on forever.

All of them influenced me as I began to see music as an important way to communicate ideas and feelings.

Bob Gibson and Bob Camp were one of the earliest and best duets at the Wha? They were a solid folksinging team whose song "To Be a Man" should be heard by everyone in every generation, but you will have a hard time finding any of their music except in rare record shops. Bob Camp, incidentally, changed his name to Hamilton Camp and became a successful actor.

Noel Stookey, on the other hand, was singing solo several nights a week at the Gaslight and Bitter End cafes in the Village until he was introduced to Mary Travers and Peter Yarrow by Albert Grossman, who would soon become the manager of many Village-based talents, including Odetta and Bob Dylan. In a few years Noel would adopt his middle name—Paul—and the popular folk group Peter, Paul, and Mary would be born, which Grossman also managed. Thirty million albums later (and a seven-year break for solo work) these three wonderful voices are still performing together. At the time, I could never have imagined that I would get to play many festivals with them through the years.

Even though poets like John Brent and Hugh Romney (who later became known as Wavy Gravy when he set up the People's Kitchen in Haight-Ashbury) are rarely seen in print today, they were a strong part of the early Village club scene and a direct link to the beatnik years that put the Village on the map as an artists' paradise and a stronghold for the anti-establishment movement. Brent, in particular, wrote outrageously funny, surrealistic poetry that challenged the mind and the soul.

Dave Van Ronk definitely was someone you had to see and hear in those days. What a great traditional folk guitarist! And his amazing raspy voice was like a dredge bringing up emotions that felt familiar to everyone. I especially liked his versions of "Down and Out," "Twelve Gates to the City," and "Cocaine Blues." Each was truly unique, like a one-act play! Fortunately, Dave's still out there traveling and singing and still great, one of the best folk/blues singers of our times.

Tim Hardin was around the early Village scene too, but most people only know his songs from the recordings of Bobby Darin and Rod Stewart, who had huge hits much later with "If I Were a Carpenter" and "Reason to Believe," respectively. Although a few Tim Hardin albums are still in print, Tim did a whole lot of fine songs that never were given the chance to make the pop charts. Many were never even recorded. I spent many nights sitting in the Night Owl Cafe listening to Tim. He played and sang melodic ballads that had haunting qualities, songs like "Hang on to a Dream." A deep sadness accompanied his voice and his songwriting throughout his short life.

I remember one very unusual night at the Night Owl when Tim Hardin was about to go on. The Night Owl was only about eighteen to twenty feet wide in certain places and the stage was situated near the front, the widest part of the joint. It had one walk-through aisle for the waitresses to serve the customers and most seats were against the wall lengthwise facing the stage, with a few tables in the front and more facing the far side of the stage in rows. That night a couple of rowdy guys came and sat at the table that abutted the front of the stage. They were kind of loaded and a bit loud. Joe Marra, the owner, asked them to keep it down. Joe didn't play around. He had a good thing going and no one was going to upset his club's atmosphere.

The guys thought that that was a bit funny. No one was on, so what was the big deal? Just as they settled in, Joe introduced Tim.

"Ladies and gentlemen, Mr. TIM HARDIN."

I was sitting back against the wall facing the stage with the backs of these guys' heads right in front of me and the aisle between us. At that point Tim was moving slowly through the aisle around a waitress and just as he got behind these guys, one of them said, "*Tim Hardin? Who the hell is Tim Hardin?*"

Standing right behind the guy, Tim gave him a very surprising slap on the back of his head. Everybody heard it and the guy, very surprised by this, turned to look up right into Tim's face, at which time he said, "I'm Tim Hardin, man. *I'm* Tim Hardin," then proceeded to climb the stairs to the stage, with the guy still rubbing his head.

Tim sat down, played one song, and went into a long dissertation on a sci-fi book he thought these guys should read—it was called *Limbo*—and then he sang one more song and left. The next day I went out and found that book, which turned out to be an incredible story by Bernard Wolfe about a future when all peoples were workers and had all been outfitted with the tools they worked with as their permanent limbs. Hammers and saws for hands and so on . . . In some way, I thought after that incident that I was able to see a deeper part of Tim Hardin. A glimpse perhaps of the future he felt we were headed for.

Eric Andersen, whose most popular tune of the day was a road song called "Thirsty Boots," often played the Gaslight. So did soft-singing Tom Paxton and Tom Rush and a rapid-fire acoustic guitarist named Danny Kalb, who did duets with Van Ronk and the great Phil Ochs before Danny helped put together the short-lived but electrifying Blues Project in the late 1960s. Andersen—one of my favorite solo performers from the early Village years—still is out there doing clubs and festivals all over the world. But you can go up and down the radio dial all day without hearing anything he's ever done.

The great Pete Seeger certainly was around. But even then, Pete was part of the older generation of folksingers, which is amazing when you think that he's still performing courageous songs about war and peace, freedom, and the environment more than half a century after he made his Carnegie Hall debut with the Weavers.

Buffy Sainte-Marie, a true Native American, was also there long before she went to Nashville or wrote "Up Where We Belong," the Oscar-winning theme to *An Officer and a Gentleman*. Buffy also wrote "Universal Soldier," a hit for Donovan and Glen Campbell, and "Until It's Time For You To Go," a hit for Elvis Presley. Later, she would show up regularly on

"Sesame Street," which I too eventually would appear on a couple of times.

Odetta was in the Village too. "The Queen of Folk Music," Odetta became a lifelong friend and personal influence whose powerful, luxurious voice sang out on behalf of solo women performers when that was not the most popular thing to be. Odetta sang songs of the people and told wonderful stories. She was not just a singer, she was an educator, and the way she effortlessly performed that dual role made a strong impression on me.

I have to tell you that it feels important for me to remember here in print some of these singers and songwriters who have been mostly forgotten in the crush of popular music. All were great natural talents who influenced every artist who passed through the Village, including the Lovin' Spoonful, José Feliciano, Jimi Hendrix, Mama Cass Elliot of the Mamas and the Papas, even Dylan and the others who gained greater fame and fortune.

One early Village performer in particular who had a major impact on *me* was someone I am sure you've never heard of: Casey Anderson.

He was an African American—one of few black folksingers in the Village—and he was a very big man, with a football player's build. Casey made you laugh a little when you first saw him onstage, because he had a tiny Martin guitar that looked like a ukulele in his oversized arms. But after Casey strapped that little axe high on his shoulder and began to sing, you knew you were in the presence of a master.

Casey loved folk ballads from Europe and the American West. He was a hypnotic figure onstage, with a beautiful voice, and he understood what to do with a song just like Sinatra understood. To Casey, like Dave Van Ronk, every song was a one-act play.

Casey knew the importance of letting your audience in on your song's secret, to visualize the beginning, the middle, and the end of the story as it develops. I loved the way Casey sang "Lily of the West," a folk ballad with a great story. Even though I had yet to begin playing guitar, I knew that I would eventually have to learn that song from him, a song that was also an early favorite of Joan Baez and was on her excellent second album.

Casey had a pure sound with a very wide range and he also had great musical timing. Even though he was much better than most of the Village singers, he was one of several early Village talents who sort of disappeared from view before the big record companies realized there was money in folk music. But if you look hard enough in old record shops, you just might find an obscure, out-of-print Casey Anderson recording. If you do, don't hesitate to get in touch with me through the publisher of this book. I would love to hear him again.

The same is true for Major Wiley, another African American, who sang with a distinct vibrato and was another one of the stars in the Village when I first came to town. Wiley, who lives and still tours in Europe and sometimes shows up in New York, was folk music's answer to pop music's Johnnie Ray.

Johnnie Ray made a career tearing off his tie and faking a

crying routine while he sang one of his hit torch songs on Milton Berle's TV show. But Wiley couldn't help bawling whenever he sang "Nora's Done," or "Fare Thee Well," or a sad love song from Appalachia. Major Wiley was a trip, but his tears were real.

I remember Carolyn Hester, who was one of the first to use Dylan as a mouth harp player and later would greatly help the development of country/folk singer Nanci Griffith. And I remember a fellow who was simply called Marcellus, the first man I ever saw with "dreadlocks," the hair style later popularized by the Rastafarians. Marcellus also was an African American who stepped up on folk stages and knocked people out with classical pieces for Spanish guitar. Marcellus and Dino Valenti were best friends. They never went anywhere without each other. They had deep love and mutual respect for each other, the rarest display of true brotherhood I'd ever seen. It was something I thought Kenny Schneider and I were developing, but we never really got the opportunity. Marcellus and Dino would become my guides to the future in many ways, the future of committed communication between fellow men.

Lotus Weinstock, whose real name was Maury Hayden, was another rare talent who surprised people everyday. Among other things, she was a brilliant comedian and was Lenny Bruce's girlfriend for a time and I believe the only partner Lenny ever worked with onstage. Later, as Lotus Weinstock, she wrote beautiful songs with sensitive lyrics, like the rarely played "Cautiously," which impressed me so much I later performed the only version ever recorded.

RICHIE HAVENS

In the 1970s, Lotus became an earth mother to many artists and musicians on the West Coast, while her daughter Lilith became a child prodigy playing classical viola at the age of
four. Lilith, still an amazing musician, wrote plays with her
mother before Lotus passed away a few years ago. She was one
of my best friends and a fine poet of the highest order.

Few people remember that Mama Cass Elliot was a Village
legend, singing beautiful folk ballads at two, three, and four
clubs a night long before she and Denny Doherty met Michelle
and John Phillips to form the Mamas and the Papas, who
moved out West for their incredible run of hit songs.

The move not only led to the breakup of the Mugwumps—
which was the band she and Denny were in—but to the forma-
tion of another major group of the 1960s, the Lovin' Spoonful,
when Zal Yanofsky, formerly of the Mugwumps, hooked up
with John Sebastian.

Sebastian played a great blues harp and auto harp for years
in the Village before he formed the Spoonful with Yanofsky,
Steve Boone, and Joe Butler at the Night Owl. Sebastian's folk
music foundation certainly helped the Spoonful become one
of the most popular American bands during the Beatles era and
I still remember John's great harmonica work in the early days.

There were so many extraordinary talents in circulation,
exchanging musical ideas and songs twenty-four hours a day.
We barely slept and when we did, it usually was after jamming—on our own time—on pillows on the floor of the Cock
and Bull or at someone's pad on MacDougal Street whenever
someone could afford to rent one.

John Mitchell, the owner of the original Gaslight Cafe, also keeps flashing across my mind. There were nights you would have to step over him sleeping on the floor to get to the door. And there were nights when he would feed six or seven of us and let us sleep in the Gaslight, rather than send us out to the street.

I also vividly remember Judy Henske, a willowy tall, majestically beautiful, passionate folksinger who performed often at Gerde's Folk City and gave one of the greatest single performances I have ever seen.

It was a set of ten songs filled with love and love gone wrong, all written by Bob Dylan, who is rarely appreciated for his songs about love, even though he has written some of the most dramatic love songs in this century. ("Boots of Spanish Leather," "Just Like a Woman," "Don't Think Twice, It's All Right," and "Girl from the North Country" are four that quickly come to mind.) Judy sang all of her songs that night in a basement coffeehouse by candlelight, wearing a slinky long evening gown with a spectacular crystal brooch on her bosom that sent the spotlight flickering back hypnotically all over the room. Every time she sang a note or moved her graceful body gently to the rhythms of the music, she sent reflected lights cascading from one side of the room to the other. It was spellbinding, a first-time-ever *light show*. A one-time-only performance, never to be repeated again.

I searched every record store in the Village for a record by Judy and almost gave up when I did something we never usually did. I went uptown. You know, past 14th Street, which was like crossing into a different time zone. Anyway, I finally did track down one of her albums, with no liner notes, no songs listed. But I bought it anyway.

It was very good, but I was really disappointed when I put it on my record player and realized it didn't have a single Dylan song on it. Not one. I was really brought down. (It turned out she never recorded them.) Still, there was a lot to listen to on that album and to this day I still play "High Flying Bird" in concert.

Dino Valenti was a strangely shy, haunting performer, who wrote many extraordinary songs, including the amazing "Get Together." which was a big hit for the Youngbloods.

Almost hypnotic onstage, Dino loved to write and make music, but was extremely turned off by the recording process just as much as he hated publicity. In fact, he strongly resisted the idea of recording so much that he just went through the motions with the two solo albums he made in the early sixties, neither of which was released. Even later, when Dino moved to the West Coast to become a founding member and major songwriter for the Quicksilver Messenger Service—one of the top groups of the psychedelic rock era—he would insist on limiting his truly unique guitar work.

Dino was intense, fascinating, and on the cutting edge of self-exploration and self-discovery that was so much a part of the consciousness-raising culture of the 1960s. There is a story I like to tell about him that probably reveals his unique intensity as much as the temperament of the times.

Dino was sitting on Muscle Beach in Venice, California,

under the parallel bars in the sand in the late 1950s, playing a single note on his guitar for two and a half hours straight—yes, a *single* note for *two and a half hours*—when a huge body-builder walked over to him and said, "Hey, man, you've been playin' that note for two hours. What's wrong with you? Don't you know anything else?"

Dino looked at the huge man for several seconds of silence with the solemnity of a Gregorian monk. Then he said, "Hey, man, don't you know . . . Don't you know there are lots of people out there desperately trying to find *this one note I'm playin'?*"

Whew!

Sometimes Dino Valenti would say and do things that would leave you thinking for a very long time.

During the early days, Dino also teamed up with Fred Neil for some of the best music ever played at the Cafe Wha? Where Dino was electrifying, Fred had a rich baritone voice that could reach into your soul.

All somebody had to say was "Neil and Valenti are playing tonight" and the in-crowd would drop everything to be there, especially to see them close out the show with their folk rock version of Ray Charles's "What'd I Say."

Picture this. As Fred and Dino were closing in on the final verse, they would keep the song going like gospel singers, marching off stage down the aisles, thrusting their guitars in the air, heading right out the back door. The packed house always screamed for more . . . And they got it.

A minute or so after they disappeared out the back door

of the Wha?—as the cheering began to die down—the voices of these two great singers could be faintly heard (as they rushed around the building) to come back inside through the front entrance, singing, "Tell me what'd I say," "Yeah, tell me what'd I say." Singing all the way, they would dance their way down the center aisle back up onstage, where they would play on for another fifteen minutes.

They were just a couple of contemporary folkies, completely involved in the music of their youth and writing the music of our future. To this day I can still see and hear Neil and Valenti coming down that center aisle, raising the roof of the Wha?, "tearing down the walls" that were keeping me from expressing what I needed to do.

Dino may have been wise beyond his years, a phenomenal musical talent, and the person who most influenced me to play the guitar in the rhythmic way I do, but Fred Neil's influence on my music and so many others was enormous and it's worth going into more detail.

The first time I saw Fred he was in a duet with Vince Martin. An accomplished studio musician at the time, Fred had already played on many hit records during the 1950s. And Vince had a number one hit with the Tarriers in the mid-fifties called "Cindy, Oh Cindy," a tune with a Caribbean flavor.

They sang Neil's "Tear Down the Walls" like the rebels they were and they made an album together on which this was the featured song. "Tear Down the Walls" was more than a good tune. It was the first protest song I ever heard in the Village, the first to point me in a clear direction. The lyrics

challenged everyone to reach beyond the barriers of their per-
ceived limitations and the prejudice of others. I could not get
enough of these two guys. They were my musical gurus in my
early days in the Village.

Watching and listening to Fred play, I knew there was a
whole big musical world out there I had never seen before. He
was a superior guitarist who knew dozens of ways to play any
major or minor chord, as well as all the sevenths and fifths.
Fred also put plenty of *suspended* chords into his music, which
he borrowed from traditional bluegrass and jazz. It's easy to
explain a suspended chord, but not easy to play. They're made
by picking and strumming parts of two different chords at the
same time. When I first saw Fred do that and heard his rich
harmonic sounds, it blew my mind.

All of us who grew up on doo-wop music and straight rock
'n' roll know that most songs can be built on simple three-
and four-chord progressions. Most folk music was also played
that way. ("Where Have All the Flowers Gone" and "500
Miles" are prime examples.) But just as the Beatles would dem-
onstrate a few years later, there was no rule that said rock 'n'
roll or folk music couldn't use the sophisticated chord structures of bluegrass or jazz.

Fred Neil understood that better than most of us. He knew
we were weaving a tapestry of many musical traditions, turning them inside out and upside down. While most of us were
picking things up as we went along, Fred was pulling things
together and inventing new directions. His songs had a won-

derful simplicity and balance to the ear, but they were built on a complex range of subtle chord combinations.

While all of Fred's recorded works were out of print for decades, two albums were combined into a poorly distributed compilation late in 1998. Some of the tracks listed below sound as fresh today as they did when he made them more than thirty years ago. Fred was—and is—one of the finest singer-songwriters this country has ever produced.

- "Little Bit of Rain," one of the best ballads to come out of the 1960s, even though it has been sparingly played or heard since Fred wrote it.
- "Other Side of This Life," recorded by many groups, including the Lovin' Spoonful; Dion; Jefferson Airplane; the Youngbloods; and Peter, Paul, and Mary.
- "The Dolphins," a lament for a real dolphin that's on my own *Live at the Cellar Door* album. It's a love song, but it was born out of Fred's wandering spirit and deep devotion to the endangered sea mammal. In fact, Fred spent several years working with dolphins in Florida after he dropped out of music.
- "Everybody's Talkin,'" the movie theme for *Midnight Cowboy* that Harry Nilsson made into a top-ten hit.
- "Blues on the Ceiling" and "The Bag I'm In," two great tunes that probably have not been heard on the radio in thirty-five years.
- "Candy Man," a great rocking tune that became one of Roy Orbison's most popular concert songs.

None of these songs were strictly folk songs—or rock songs. They were just great to sing, great to play, and great to listen to. They still are. The truth is that Fred was a major influence on everybody in the Village music scene and probably would have been among the most recognized singer-songwriters in the world, if two things hadn't happened to him.

He got screwed terribly by a lot of people in the music industry. And like so many artists under siege from the insincerity of the business, Fred took a wrong turn to hard drugs out of deep despair and nearly lost his life.

Today Fred is completely at peace with himself, having spent years working through things, far away from the music scene in Coconut Grove, Florida, and New York City. In the last few years, he has even spent some time hanging out with Jerry Jeff Walker in the Northwest, playing now and then strictly for friends. All of us who knew him back in the old days are proud that he's made it through some very tough times. While few people in today's music world have any clue what they missed, the music he made is still there. Even more importantly, Fred and I are friends for life and beyond.

catching 1,000 rising stars

One of the things that surprised me about the Village was the incredible range of comedy in the clubs. During the 1960s, you could see most of the great comedic talents of our lifetime in the Village. Most of them were just starting out.

I saw Richard Pryor's and Bill Cosby's first performances in the Village. Rodney Dangerfield got his start there. So did Joan Rivers and Vaughn Meader, who impersonated President Kennedy better than anyone in Kennedy's family and contributed to the sense of good humor most people associate with the Kennedy presidency. Actor Ed Lauder also got his start as a comedian there and few people who see him performing his character bits in serious films have any idea just how funny Ed's incredibly accurate impressions of "sounds of real life" were. I can truly say after watching Ed at least sixty times that he was one of the very best.

David Steinberg began in the Village, and from time to time you would see David Brenner or the veteran comedians Mort Sahl and Myron Cohen show up as well. The humor was sometimes political, sometimes biting, in the satiric tradition pioneered in the Village by Lenny Bruce in the 1950s. Or it was sharply aimed at exposing our human failings, so we could see ourselves as we really are.

One of the most brilliant comedians I saw back then was Jody Graber, who died in the early eighties, still trying to make it.

Jody had no manager and never got a real TV break but was such a naturally funny man who used his own experiences as his comic routines on the streets of the Village every day.

Jody had a dog named Star who went with him everywhere, always eight feet behind, or to the side, or in front of him, moving on cue whenever Jody looked over in his direction. They were a funny pair to meet on the street and Jody wouldn't hesitate to bring Star onstage at the Wha? After finishing his bit, he'd turn to Star and say, "Okay, Star, it's your turn." The dog would quickly wake up from a deep sleep, then leap over Jody's arm as they walked offstage together.

Jody broke everybody up with a bit from his Navy days. He'd start out talking about hitchhiking on leave and say, "You know, I'm convinced state troopers have a special radar machine that can detect a thumb in the air at a five-mile range . . . If not, how come every time I raise mine for a ride— *zoom*—a trooper is right on me with handcuffs. And when I do get lucky and get a ride, why do I always wind up with a guy who stays silent for fifteen minutes until he leans over to place a hand on my leg and says with a high-pitched voice, 'So tell me now, do you like sports?' Thanks a lot."

Jody did a long, very funny routine about being scared as a kid after he'd been to a midnight horror movie at the local bijou when horror movies only played at midnight. "I found out," Jody said, "that a coat hanging inside the front door, casting a shadow in the dark, is the best laxative man's ever invented."

Jody said he'd run upstairs, jump into bed, and pull the covers over his head until he couldn't hold his water anymore. Then he'd tiptoe down the stairs to the kitchen and stare across the foyer that led to the bathroom before he got enough courage up to raise his voice and announce for anyone within five blocks to hear: "I'M GOING TO THE BATHROOM NOW AND . . . AND . . . AND . . . I'VE GOT A SHARP KNIFE AND FORK IN MY HAND . . ."

"God forbid something would jump out of the dark at me," Jody would conclude. Then he would mime stabbing himself, suddenly running as if he were running straight through the second-story wall.

Jody Graber did not wind up on the Broadway stage or as a regular guest on *The Tonight Show*. Jody wound up as a private garbage collector.

As a garbage collector, Jody saw dollar signs on some of the things people threw away. He was a connoisseur of high-quality things. Jody collected televisions, radios, and Oriental rugs that proved to be worth several thousand dollars apiece.

Jody actually was able to buy a house and retire to Florida on the money he made—not as a comedian, but from what he found on the street. True story!

Greenwich Village was more than clubs and comedians and coffeehouses. It was New York University, which brought thousands of students and teachers from all over the world to my new neighborhood. It was great old brownstone buildings and curiosity shops, old record stores, ethnic restaurants, and movie houses playing foreign or obscure films. It was dozens of outdoor cafes where you could watch people and write or read for hours. And it was Washington Square Park.

The park was a great place to hang out; it was more than a meeting place or even a private resting place. It was Greenwich Village Central, one of the great spots in the Western world.

There were folk and jazz singers, marimba bands, yo-yo champs, and magicians. There were kids playing Frisbee with their dads. Moms watching their preschoolers climb monkey bars a few feet from world-class chess hustlers with time clocks.

From dawn to sunset, so many memorable characters found their way in and out of the park.

There were the mimes who gave Broadway-class performances in midafternoon near the archway at the north end of the park. There was a juggler who looked like Jesus, complete with the long hair that would become so popular by the mid-sixties, and there was the gay couple who walked their two toy dogs on the same route through the park every day at the same exact time. There were hundreds of characters in the park.

Big Brown, who was close to seven feet tall and built like Atlas, was always there. If you were there too, I am sure you remember him. He was an ex-sparring partner for former heavyweight boxing champion Ezzard Charles.

Every day Big Brown scared the daylights out of people just by staring at them. He would stand alone for an hour or two—still as a stone—near one of the corner entrances as if he was standing guard. But he would stare at the sky until people gathered all around him. Many did. And when they were totally engrossed, Big Brown would suddenly turn toward them and *roar* like a lion, knocking several of them to the ground. And with a growling, rumbling voice, he would shout: "Get *up*, GET UP OFF *MY EARTH!*"

Sometimes Big Brown showed another side of himself in the park. Sometimes you might find him standing on top of the pedestal of the fountain in the center of the park, reciting Edgar Allan Poe's great poem "The Raven"—word for word— in all its chilling intensity. Big Brown was much more than a very large man with muscles and a powerful demeanor. He had a world of interests and he knew how to captivate a crowd.

Tony McKay, a singer from the West Indies, also enter- tained a lot of people in the park. McKay was surrounded by people whenever he pulled out his guitar and laid his case open on the ground. He was pleasant enough singing familiar tunes, but the crowds doubled and tripled whenever McKay jumped into some of his exciting Caribbean rhythms. The park got very lively when Tony McKay did his thing. Actually, I was blown away by how many truly great musicians played this park for nickels and dimes. Not many ever made much of an impact nationally, mostly because they actually seemed to need or prefer a low-key street musician's life. Yet some were as good as you would hear anywhere in the city.

Joe the Policeman was in the park every day too. He was an old-fashioned cop who patrolled MacDougal Street and the park and helped everybody in the Village, including the store-keepers, artists, and the homeless. Joe even called the parents of kids in the neighborhood after dark to let them know that their runaway teenage daughters and sons were on their way home. And if one of these kids got into trouble, Joe was the kind of caring person who would go out of his way to find out what was happening at home and what was in the kid's head. This was way-different than any cop I had seen before. Until Joe, the only cops I saw in action were corrupt and arrogant ones, like the ones I left behind in Brooklyn and at least one I ran into on a subway platform in the Village.

I was walking through the turnstiles in the 4th Street station, about a block from the park, when I saw a young black man being arrested at gunpoint near the end of the platform. It was a quiet time of day and after watching what was going on for a minute, I couldn't just stand there without moving closer and saying something.

"What did the kid do?" I asked in a normal speaking voice. "Why do you have him at gunpoint?"

"None of your damn business," the cop said. "Shut your mouth and let me see some ID. "

Wrong thing to say to me.

"First of all, Officer, " I said. "I only asked you a simple question, so there's no reason to talk to me like that. Now I really would like to know what this is all about. You work *for me*, you know. I pay your salary!"

Wrong thing to say to him.

"So you want an *answer,* do you? Eh, wise guy? Then move your blankety-blank over here and put your hands behind your back . . . *YOU'RE UNDER ARREST.*"

He wasn't kidding. Within minutes I went from being a bystander who wanted to know what was going on to having handcuffs snapped on my wrists. I couldn't believe it and I kept saying so. It turned out I was right. The only thing the kid had done was jump the turnstile. The policeman didn't have to pull his gun on him.

But that didn't matter. An hour later, I was on my way to a two-week stay in the Harts Island jail for disorderly conduct.

I could've called my family, but I had left home to make my own way. So when the judge said fourteen days, I resigned myself to it and just went with the flow. Sometimes I am too curious for my own good.

The consolation for my trouble was meeting people and hearing their stories in jail, people in an uphill climb toward a decent life who had been slapped down again and again. Harts Island was for offenders who had too many car tickets, or were months behind in their support payments, or were in for disorderly conduct, which is what I was charged with. There were plenty of real people in trouble in that jail and some were caught in the violence of the street too.

One man had five serious wounds from bullets in his chest, along with five exit wounds in his back. Just looking at him up close made me realize just how resilient our human body must be to withstand that kind of attack. Or how strong the human spirit can be when survival is at stake.

This certainly was a world much different than the open, creative one I was getting exposed to in the Village. But it was a world I had gotten glimpses of before, a world that was being brought to the surface in the new songs of protest and freedom being written and sung all around me.

7

from portraits to songs

I had endless energy. Still do. But once or twice a week I'd check into the Albert Hotel, just to get a full night's sleep. The rest of the week I'd hit Washington Square Park in the morning, the Cafe Wha? all day for music, do portraits for a bunch of hours at night, and then drop over to the Night Owl Cafe on 4th Street for conversation and french fries and gravy till three in the morning. An hour or two of sleep and I'd start my cycle all over again. There was too much going on out there for me to sleep. But I wasn't Superman.

One Saturday during my second Village winter, I had been up for four straight days and it all caught up with me. I was so tired I practically crawled over to the Albert to crash before nightfall. Man, was I beat.

When I woke, I couldn't believe that it was still dark outside. I felt cheated, but I was too restless to stay in bed. So I got dressed and went down to the gallery to do some portraits.

As soon as I walked in the door, the owner jumped out from behind a stack of boxes and yelled at me, "WHERE THE BLANKETY-BLANK WHERE YOU?"

"I was *here*. Yesterday," I said.

"The heck you were," he said. And we argued back and forth about it until he suddenly stopped and asked me with a strange look on his face: "What in the blankety-blank day do you think this is, Richie?"

"Saturday," I said.

"Bull-oney, " he said. "It's not even Sunday; it's MONDAY, Richie. Monday night!"

I was so tired that I had slept all the way through the weekend. It was five-thirty on Monday evening and I had slept forty-four hours straight!

There went my portrait gig.

He didn't want to take the chance that it would happen again. All he could see was the money he would lose; it made him crazy.

But all things happen for a reason. For just a short while longer, I would continue to do portraits in front of the park and on Sixth Avenue, where some of my friends also set up shop. Occasionally I would go back to Brooklyn to bring some money home and sketch some people I knew. In fact, my most important portrait turned out to be one of my last ones—on a trip back to Brooklyn.

On Eastern Parkway I saw a poster for SMOKEY ROBINSON AND THE MIRACLES PLAYING TODAY at a nearby place called Town Hill. Smokey was a huge star, a role model for a lot of young black singers, especially if you grew up in Brooklyn and had any music in you. One look at the poster pushed me right to Town Hill in the middle of the afternoon.

I sneaked upstairs to the ballroom, where I found myself all alone watching a full band rehearsal, an amazing performance. Afterward Smokey came down off the stage to ask me, the stranger, what I was holding so tightly under my arm. I showed him my portrait book and he rushed me backstage to draw his wife Claudette, who was part of the group.

At the time I thought meeting Smokey and doing his wife's portrait was the highlight of my life. But it was just the flash point for my transition into music. Back in the Village, I didn't feel like doing portraits or reading poetry as much. Watching Smokey perform made me hear the voice inside me that was pushing me toward making my own music. Smokey was a fine singer-songwriter whose lyrics seemed more poetic than most on the pop charts. Suddenly I wanted to really see and hear all the great Village singers and musicians. Suddenly I wanted to sing every great song I had been hearing for the last two years. Songs that taught me something new or made me think about things I never considered before. Songs that were changing me and my life.

I had a guitar. Had it for quite a while. About a year and a half after I first came to the Village, a friend of mine who saw me fooling around with one of his guitars gave it to me as a gift. It was a handmade instrument with a good sound and I regret that I lost it several years later somewhere along the road. It deserved a better fate. Even though I would not really use it for almost two years, I instinctively knew when I got it that it would open a new voice for me, a voice from within that I had never really heard before.

Turned on by so many things, especially the music of Fred Neil and Dino Valenti, I began to take this guitar with me every day to a quiet bench in a corner of Washington Square Park—to teach myself how to play. For a while, I thought the most comfortable way for me to play was to lay the guitar across my lap like a dulcimer.

In the early 1960s you could find twenty to thirty traditional and contemporary folksingers in the park playing all kinds of acoustic instruments, wailing away, passing the hat to make a living doing what they loved to do. To entertain and educate the tourists who came to the Village in search of the legendary beatniks they had heard so much about.

I watched Tony McKay make his chord changes and tried to copy them, but got tired trying all the different finger positions. I almost gave up until I experimented with a completely different way of playing.

My Open Tuning Bar Chord Method

Instead of placing my fingers in the right places on the right strings to make traditional chords, I changed the tuning of a few strings to make a complete chord without pressing down on the fret board at all. By tuning the guitar in this way—to an "open chord"—and by strumming all six strings together, it took me all of ten seconds to realize I could slide my thumb along the neck of the guitar to make different chords at every fret stop.

This resembled a technique used in playing "bottleneck" blues guitar, but it was not what they were teaching in guitar classes. It was, however, much, much easier than anything I saw happening. In fact, I wonder how many young musicians out there today could get into their own music a lot quicker using my "open tuning bar chord method," which I thought you might like to see a bit closer. By tuning the guitar this way and playing two or three chords in sequence, you will have all the background harmony you need to sing hundreds of songs.

The tuning for each of the six strings—from the top bass string down, is: D, A, D, F#, A, D. And the picture below will show you how to begin.

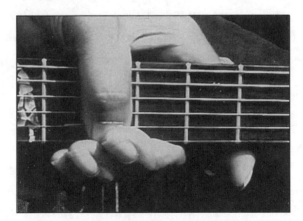

Open D Suspensions

In this configuration, which is almost identical to the first one, I use my thumb as the tool to change the basic major

chords while leaving the bottom two or three strings open. Try this fingering on all of the frets—one fret at a time, first leaving two strings open. See which ones sound good to you. I should tell you that most of the chords I play, I play this way. I leave just two strings open. But there is at least one fret where I leave three strings open. You might want to find it yourself. It creates a B minor suspended chord.

Reverse Suspensions

The fingering in the following photo allows a suspended open D chord while you change the root notes of the chord to effect subtle key changes. Try using this fingering for each and every fret. Find the ones that work for you. You will discover great sounds to incorporate into songs you might be learning.

These are just a few configurations that I use to play the way I do. But it shouldn't be hard to sing a large number of rock 'n' roll or folk songs with the few I've shown you. Have fun!

RICHIE HAVENS

Playing the guitar in this relaxed, open style brought me a lot closer to accompanying songs I already knew. And the harmonies that traveled from the instrument back to my ears gave me a flood of new words, melodies, and musical ideas. That is what playing a musical instrument can do for anyone. When you make music, it actually feeds on itself and inspires more music. And if you think that this is some rare gift that only a select few of us have, you're wrong. *Everybody* has good music in them. It's basic human equipment.

Some people tell me that they really get into my strumming rhythms. For some reason, it became automatic for me to play with enough rhythm in order for me to sing—to fill in the spaces my voice needed to feel supported—and I never consciously paid too much attention to working on that part of my music. It developed almost without notice.

When I learned a song, I automatically felt the tempo to sing it; the strumming was there to fill in the gaps between lines and to emphasize anticipations, pickups, and turnarounds. The other odd thing was that my left foot became my body metronome. I tapped it heel to toe, which gave me a rhythm to play the guitar against. I guess you could say that my own foot took the place of a drummer (or bass player), who holds down the basic rhythm in a band so that other instruments have the freedom to play melody or counterrhythmic licks. In my case, my natural rhythm was coming from my foot right through my body so that I could sing the songs that were changing my life.

From the time I was very young I was always able to hear the separate notes in any played chord or any complicated melody and was able to sing them back when my music teacher asked me to. I truly believe I inherited this from my father's ability to play the piano by ear. My mother, on the other hand, had a wonderful voice, but she sang only when she was washing dishes or mopping the floor. The song I remember loving to hear her sing was "Red Sails in the Sunset," a beautiful ballad that was very popular when I was very young.

Between my father's genetic gift to me and my mother's love of beautiful melodies, I think it was a foregone conclusion that music was in my blood, not that I was going to really be privileged to play and sing professionally. You cannot imagine how much I am still amazed that I am doing just that.

live in new york city

anging out in the park and going to the Cafe Wha? every night brought me closer and closer toward bringing my guitar onstage.

I learned "Tear Down the Walls," Fred Neil's compelling protest song that I had ringing in my head, and I learned a great rocking blues tune he wrote: "The Bag I'm In."

I would sing these songs in the park whenever I was sure Fred wasn't there. And if you ever heard Fred sing and play, you'd know exactly why I was shy about doing them in front of him.

Len Chandler, a fine folk blues singer, pulled me onstage one night to trade a few verses at the Gaslight. Chandler had heard me read my poetry at the Cock and Bull. He pulled me right out of the audience in the middle of his set.

Even after that, it took me ten more months before I gained the courage to do a set of songs onstage—on a "hoote-

(*from left*): Lou Gossett Jr., Taj Mahal, Len Chandler, and some guy with a great big grin. (*Photo by Leslie Hawes*)

nanny night," an open-mike night for performers. The songs were pushing me toward performing. They were expressing missing truths or telling stories that helped people see themselves and each other more clearly.

In those days all the singers in the Village took time to explain something about their songs, where they came from, or who was enduring what when they were written, or why they deserved to be heard.

For instance, a very old folk tune like "The Bells of Rhymney," which you might know from Roger McGuinn's recording with the Byrds, was one of the songs I sang in my earliest appearances onstage. It spoke to a history that went much deeper than anything we had been taught in school.

The song was about coal miners and mine owners in Wales and it told how the church bells would ring through the town when a mine had caved in. The song revealed feelings of people who endured the hazards of living such a hard, uncertain life in unsafe conditions. It was, in its own lyrical way, as revealing as Woody Guthrie's Depression-era songs.

THE BELLS OF RHYMNEY

O what will you give me
Say the sad bells of Rhymney

Is there hope for the future
Cry the brown bells of Merthyr

Who made the mine owner
Say the black bells of Rhondda
And who robbed the miner
Cry the grim bells of Blaina

They will plunder willy-nilly
Cry the bells of Caerphilly
They have fangs, they have teeth
Say the loud bells of Neathe

69

THEY CAN'T HIDE US ANYMORE

Even God is uneasy
Say the moist bells of Swansea
Put the vandals in court
Say the bells of Newport

All would be well if, if, if
Cry the green bells of Cardiff

Why so worried, sisters, why
Sang the silver bells of Wye
And what will you give me
Say the sad bells of Rhymney

When I listened to songs like that, songs that had strong melodic lines and yet told real stories, I would hear more than pure, beautiful music, I would hear the *under*history of a people, the history that revealed a universal truth about a land, or a time, or a group of people who resembled our neighbors, ourselves, our friends.

I felt close to songs like that, songs that are still worth singing. Once I discovered them, I began to sense my true calling . . . the communications business. This was strongly reinforced early on in my passing the basket days, the night I attended my first "real concert" outside the Village.

Often I would see a young man come into the Cafe Wha?, usually with different people. He was a cousin of Neil Sedaka, who was at his peak at the time. One Saturday the young man brought a lady with him, also his cousin, and after my set she asked me if I had ever heard of Josh White. I told her I had only heard his name mentioned by a few hard-core folkies. She said I reminded her of him—a lot—and encouraged me to see him perform. I didn't know when I would ever get to do that, but two weeks later she came back and generously gave me a ticket to see him in concert uptown at Hunter College. I actually took off from my nightly circle of gigs at several Village coffeehouses to go.

It was at this concert that I saw one man and his guitar on a fifty-foot stage with a black velvet curtain behind him, with one leg over the back of a chair, playing for so many people. It was incredible how he connected with the entire audience. He sang songs from the past and songs he had written about the struggles of mankind. All of them moved me.

He brought out his daughter to sing one of the most beautiful songs in the world, the famous Irish ballad "Danny Boy." It brought tears to my eyes and for the first time, I heard the story that went with this Song—*A War Story*—along with all the missing verses you never heard on the radio.

Josh White also brought out his son, who was about eight or nine years old, and they all sang together. It was a very inspiring night for me; I was never the same after that. I felt even stronger about the direction I was headed. Much later I would actually wind up playing some of the same festivals Josh played, and years after that I would do many concerts and festivals with his son, Josh White, Jr., an awesome performer himself.

These were days when those of us with guitars and songs

were coming to grips with our talents and our new voices. Most of us had just left our teenage years behind, years when we were seldom heard or listened to. Now we were on our own, without a clue or a compass, but many of us understood that something was out of whack.

We felt driven to open up tightly closed doors, to challenge sexual taboos, and to make some sense out of so much hidden nonsense. Our parents and teachers called us rebels and they were right. Our leaders didn't know what to make of us. We were rebels for the truth we felt was being kept from us.

Politicians reacted in fear to anyone who sang a song that questioned the size of the military budget or the dangerous pollution of our freshwater lakes and streams. The press barely addressed such issues truthfully; it's still rare when they do. That's why the singers of old folk music began to write about contemporary events. That's what brought both groups together in the Village clubs. That's what led to the songs becoming so popular on college campuses and on the radio. We were singing and writing about real emotions, feelings, and events, about African Americans still being denied equal citizenship, and about the way the native Indian nations were being treated. Far from dropping out, far from not caring, we were doing something I'm still proud of. We were living out the American dream. We were experiencing the freedom to reveal the establishment's secrets and lies.

Most of us grew up believing in the ideals we had been taught about America in our childhood. But we were a generation who saw the American dream being corrupted or withheld by those who swore to uphold and protect it. We wondered why our grandparents and parents, who fought World War I and World War II to preserve our freedoms, were unaware of these precious gifts slipping away. We were not anti-American. We *were* Americans.

In our own way, we were trying to promote the American ideal: the only one we knew. Through our songs, through private discovery, through one-on-one conversations with strangers and friends, through spontaneous protests of many kinds, sometimes with no political sophistication at all.

We did believe what we had been taught growing up and we felt free enough to express it until we were radicalized in the press and by our own government.

All we were seeking were ways to break through false traditional barriers and the new ones being built around us. That's what the music in the Village said. That's what we openly talked about, that's what we felt, and that's what we did individually.

9

the man who changed my life

The first song that I like to sing at most of my performances was written by a gentleman who was very special in my life. The truth is that he actually changed
my life. A great deal.

By this time, I was playing about two dozen songs in the
basement coffeehouses. They had a whole lot more going for
them than the "I love you, she loves my best friend" songs
that were flooding the airwaves. They spoke to our frustrations
over the social and political climate and to deeper connections
between people.

They certainly did something for me.

They were songs that made me think and made me see
things more clearly. So when I finally took on the guitar as
part of me, I wasn't thinking about a career; I just needed to
sing these songs for my own sense of expression, to bring them
out the way I heard them and maybe allow others to pick up

on their educational or inspirational values. The coffeehouses were strongholds for communication: underground communication.

There were a whole bunch of us doing about a dozen sets a night—from one coffeehouse to another, seven days a week—for spare change and all the coffee we could drink. There was much less money in it than drawing portraits—by far—but it was a special time, probably as stimulating to all of us performing onstage as the painters and writers who mingled together in Paris cafes during the 1920s.

For a while, I hung out with a few pretty crazy guys from the Midwest who called themselves the Tanners. Chuck Irose was the lead singer and we all shared a couple of rooms in the Broadway Central Hotel (it later collapsed) and swapped music twenty-four hours a day for several months.

It was a great time to be in Greenwich Village. We were learning so much from each other. And one of the things we all did was follow new people who showed up in town—to check them out for a new song, or a musical idea, or maybe to see if they were going to be good enough to knock us out of the box. Even in the Village, we felt the need to be good enough to get the better gigs.

People with guitars were coming to New York every day, heading straight to the Village. They would start out by playing hootenannies at the Gaslight or the Wha?, hoping to break into the rotation.

So one night a guy by the name of Gene Michaels shows up with his guitar, a guitar so beautiful that he attracted attention as soon as he walked to the stage. It was a big shiny dreadnought with spectacular abalone inlaid all over it. I was hypnotized completely by this guitar and I followed *it*—not him—from coffeehouse to coffeehouse every night for a week.

Slowly I began to realize that he had written quite a few beautiful songs. In fact, I stopped looking at the guitar long enough to hear Gene sing a song that just blew me away. I mean, it was so deep, so powerful. I knew I had to sing it.

Later that night, I didn't ask Gene if I could look at his guitar up close for the umpteenth time. Actually, he seemed more than willing to teach me the song; but the next night and the night after that, I couldn't get him to do it.

A month later, I was still waiting.

I did get a few of the verses down on my own, but it was a long song and I couldn't quite get it all. And I couldn't wait any longer. So one night when Gene finished his set, I chased him in the darkest corner of this smoke-filled, dimly lit coffeehouse and gave him a deep, long stare.

"Hey, Gene," I said slowly, "I believe *tonight* is the night you're *definitely* going to teach me that song."

For an instant, Gene actually looked a little scared and I had a hard time holding back a big laugh. But he caught on and decided to write down the lyrics. Gene went back to the kitchen and scribbled down all thirteen verses of the song.

About fifteen minutes later, he came back out and handed it to me on three half-crumpled pieces of paper. Never said a word. Picked up his guitar, walked out the door, and disappeared. I mean, he really disappeared. I never saw Gene again.

But finally I had *the song.*

So I took the three crumpled-up pieces of paper back to the Broadway Central and spent eight hours a day for three days learning the thirteen verses and working out my own arrangement.

For a month, I sang it for friends and in a couple of coffee-house sets and people reacted much as I did. It was a very moving song. Then when I got to sing at what I would call my first "legitimate" coffeehouse where people like Odetta and Pete Seeger got to play, I knew what song I was going to play. So I told the audience from the stage, "Gene Michaels wrote this song," just as I had done before singing it every time. I also told them that the song had changed me as a person and I wanted people to know who wrote *this great song.*

The audience responded wildly with almost deafening applause.

Scared the hell out of me.

Little did I realize they also were laughing.

The crowd whistled and yelled things from the back of the room that I could not make out. The electricity in the air was so intense, I ran off the stage. A few minutes later, standing in the dark behind the audience, a young man stepped up in front of me with tears coming down his face. He was moved.

"*Oh, man,*" he said, choking on his emotion, "that . . . that . . . that was my *favorite version* of that song." I could barely say thank you before I had to get away from him too. I wasn't used to this kind of reaction. "Way too heavy for me," I whispered under my breath, heading for the dressing room, which was downstairs.

Dave Van Ronk was blocking my way, waiting for me.

"Hey, man, do you know *who that was* who came over to you just now?"

I didn't have a clue. "No, I don't, " I answered.

"He wrote that song you just sang," he said.

"No, he didn't," I said. "Gene Michaels wrote that song." I was so sure.

"The *hell* he did! The *guy you just met* wrote that song," Van Ronk said firmly. And he was right; he was right.

Hell of a way to meet Bob Dylan!

For a whole month, I'd been telling everybody that somebody else wrote *his* song and then on my first night in a real coffeehouse, I get the chance to tell Dylan himself that somebody else wrote "A Hard Rain's a-Gonna Fall."

Pretty e-m-b-a-r-r-a-s-s-i-n-g. But I guess I did learn one lesson that night that was even more important. After that, I knew exactly where a lot of my songs were going to come from.

turning pro

In 1963 I met Albert Grossman after playing my fifth set in a third coffeehouse gig late one Saturday afternoon. I didn't know who he was, but every time I looked out into the audience there was this heavyset man with streaks of white-gray hair staring back at me through thick glasses. I must have seen Albert at my gigs for a month. He was always well dressed and businesslike.

Albert was the owner of a folk music cafe in Chicago called the Gate of Horn, but nobody in the Village really knew who he was until he sold the club and practically took over the whole music scene. "I think you should record some of those songs," he said ten seconds after introducing himself. "Did you ever think of doing that?"

I honestly didn't think so, not with so many really good performers on the street waiting for their chance. But he was very persuasive. He said he was looking for people to promote. He said I was one of the first he wanted to sign.

Heady stuff for a kid from Brooklyn who was just having fun and learning—not really knowing how to play for real, like the others. So heady that I couldn't say no to a trip to his New York office, where we talked about music: what I liked and didn't like. I felt as though I was being told by the Dodgers that they were going to sign me to a major league contract. Except I wasn't a kid anymore. And this wasn't exactly the Dodgers either.

Albert was an interesting, mysterious person. I had seen him many times in the backs of so many clubs and had fanta-sized about who he might be. I called him "the Continental." But he wasn't at all what I had imagined.

So I signed. Why not? If this guy was going to help me earn one more dime than I was already making, what could be wrong with that? Besides, I already had read plenty of contracts since I was fourteen years old when offers were coming in all the time for our doo-wop groups. This would be basically the same. Or so I thought.

So we recorded a few tracks in a studio. But for the next three years, every dime I made still came from my Village club dates. No gigs from Albert, no tours, no anything. I was pretty frustrated, especially while Albert seemed to be helping out just about every other talent in the Village, from Dylan to Odetta and Gordon Lightfoot to Peter, Paul, and Mary.

It wasn't all Albert's fault. I was naïve enough to believe I had signed a management contract like the others I had seen. Wrong. All I had signed was an independent *production* contract. Nothing more and a whole lot less.

Once the demos were done, it seemed Albert didn't make much of an effort to sell them to a record company, but there was no mystery about that. For some reason, he had hooked me up with different types of bands to record my songs, nothing close to what I was doing onstage. Albert was too busy to really know what to do with a guy singing all kinds of songs with an acoustic guitar. But one day he came up to my apartment in the East Village to sort of apologize and give me some advice and encouragement. Even though the rock, jazz, or country styles hadn't worked, he wasn't giving up.

"It's not quite your time yet, Richie," Grossman said. "Hang in there."

I didn't really know if Albert was telling it to me straight or sidestepping his promises. All I knew was I liked my music now. I had a few dozen songs and was playing to good crowds ten or twelve times a night in several Village clubs. I did solo gigs and played as a trio with two other young musicians who were going to be with me for a very long time.

One was Paul "Deano" Williams, a friend from my neighborhood in Brooklyn who played maracas before he decided to teach himself how to play guitar the same way I did—with the same open chord. Actually, I brought Deano into the group after I found a sixteen-year-old conga player, Daniel Alexander McCloud, who was always changing something about himself and actually changed his name a few times before he settled on Daniel Ben Zebulon. But while Daniel was figuring out what his name should be, we just called him Natoga, the first name we knew him by.

Deano has been with me from the Village days to Wood-stock right to the present. Natoga also was at Woodstock, but he went on to play with many other musicians, like the Rolling Stones and Stevie Wonder, to name just a couple. And he moved back to Florida, where he was born.

Whenever I'm in Florida, and Natoga shows up, he puts his sound right into the mix as if he never left.

The first time I saw Natoga he was playing three conga drums and doing songs from the great Olatunji's *Drums of Passion* album in the Cafe Bizarre, a huge coffeehouse carved out of the old Aaron Burr stables in the Village. He was a teenager who had run away from home. He was Gene Krupa without drumsticks and he really blew my mind when I saw him perform for the first time.

The ghost of Aaron Burr still lived in the Cafe Bizarre. I swear I saw him sitting there one day and I'm not the only one. I was running a hootenanny, coming up from the base-ment on a Saturday afternoon—after turning on the lights for the whole coffeehouse. I opened up the door to the kitchen and saw this shadowy man dressed in faded clothes out of the eighteenth century. He was just sitting there while the hair on the nape of my neck shot straight up in the air, leaving dozens of goose bumps.

The Bizarre was owned and operated by a small family and I asked them who the strange guy sitting in the corner was. "Oh, that's only Aaron," they said. "He's in there all the time."

Whew!

RICHIE HAVENS

I knew Deano's whole family. One of the kids I had brought into the Village to sing back in 1960 was Deano's youngest brother. I went to grade school with Deano's sister and with another of his brothers, Keith Williams. Keith was one of the better singers in all of Brooklyn. He sang with some of the guys who formed the Flamingos and Velores and he also worked for a while with the legendary gospel group the Soul Stirrers, which only happened to feature the great Sam Cooke, Harvey Fuqua of the Moonglows, Clyde McPhatter, and a young Teddy Pendergrass.

Deano didn't realize that he had any musical talent. He was so young and too busy trying to stay alive. Right next door to where his family lived, a woman was killed by a policeman. From her window on the top floor, she saw this cop bothering some kids who were really just being kids. The cop seemed to have some bad history with them and they were not smart enough to back off. The angered policeman chased the kids into her building and up the three flights. Tempers got hot and to distract things, the young mother came out from her apartment as the kids ran past her door and she threw a pan down the stairs. Unfortunately, it bounced wildly toward the cop, who promptly shot her dead.

That was only one of several violent incidents between the police and friends of mine in Bed-Stuy in the late fifties. Like I said, I had to get out of there and Deano, on his own at fourteen, felt exactly the same.

Not long afterward, a friendly promoter-manager—Jacob Solmon—saw us play and told me that he wanted to help.

Jacob, whose nickname was Jack, was not looking to cut in on anyone else's deal. He was young and he was collecting disability checks from the government. Jack was simply inclined to help Village performers and managers he liked, often for free. While Grossman was making barrels of money with Dylan and Peter, Paul, and Mary, Jack was out there watching and listening every night, giving friendly business guidance to folkies needing a little push. I remember him telling Peter Tork, a wonderful singer-songwriter who played banjo, "Go to California . . . New York isn't for you." Barely a week after Peter got there, he auditioned for a TV show and got it. *The Monkees!*

In 1966 Jack helped get me a job as a troubadour for an Off-Broadway production at the 73rd Street Theater in Manhattan. He thought it would be a good thing for me to do, even though it was going to be hard on me. Not because I had to act; that wasn't even part of the job. It was going to be difficult because it would cost me money.

I had to give up most of my coffeehouse gigs every night just to be in this play. The theatrical job paid only seventy-three dollars a week and all of seven dollars was taken right off the top for union dues. I had very little time to go from there to the Village to make up enough money to pay my rent. At the time, I was paying my rent by passing the hat after my sets.

The play lasted about three months and it took about two and a half months to pay off the union. Little did I know then how much I would learn about the acting profession. It turned out that I had two of the best teachers right in front of me every night. I watched James Earl Jones and Moses Gunn display some of the most arresting performances I had ever seen, not that I had seen that much theater before, but I knew I was seeing some of the best actors in the world. Most of what I learned was subliminal, but watching James and Moses do what they did best was the best teaching tool I could have had.

James was amazing, in that he always changed or added something new each night to his performance and I could see how he integrated each change so flawlessly, as if it was written that way. It really was a wonderful experience. I knew then that both James and Moses were going to become well known in their business.

The play was *Bohickee Creek*, by Robert Unger, an up-and-coming playwright at the time. Actually, it was four one-act plays that took place at different parts of a creek that emptied into the Mississippi River at a time when the South was going through great change.

I had to sing four songs, each of which was an allegory that preceded a play. The plays were done on almost bare stages with very few props. Only the platforms the actors performed on were moved around to make up the set changes for each play. I was the storyteller and that's when I sang the songs to set up the plays. The story lines were about the progress taking place in the South at different locations along Bohickee Creek in the early fifties—the knocking down of shanty shacks to make way for new housing and the displacement of those who lived there to the murder of two Klan members in the last play. This was controversial stuff at the time, but it helped people see the plight of the African American in the South. By the end of the run, I was a member of the union, not ever having acted before and not knowing how that would benefit me, since I was not going to be looking for any acting jobs. But it was around this time when I got my first chance to sing at the Newport Folk Festival in the workshops on song-writing. And at the very least, I had two very wonderful friends that made the whole experience worth it.

My Bohickee Creek experience later led to my first *real* acting job, which was playing the part of Othello in the film *Catch My Soul*, a modern musical version directed by Patrick McGoohan, produced by Metromedia, and distributed by New Line Cinema. I would also do *Greased Lightning* with Richard Pryor and would even have the pleasure of working with Moses Gunn in the movie *Perfect Harmony*.

As Jacob Solmon suggested prior to *Bohickee Creek*, there was much to be gained working with serious actors. At the very least, being a non-actor, the experiences contributed to my delivery of certain songs through the years. Many songs, in fact, have the dramatic impact of good theatrical plays.

Jack usually had good instincts about show business mat-ters and he was a courageous young man too, the first person in the Village to organize the folksingers so they would get paid—at least a little bit—instead of having to rely strictly on passing the hat.

Every coffeehouse in the Village refused to pay performers. They claimed they had no cabaret license, so they "couldn't."

RICHIE HAVENS

From Village coffeehouses to concert halls, it's still the same kind of communication. (*Photo by Mauren Brodbeck*)

But the truth was that it cost only nine dollars a year for such a license at the time.

After pointing out how unfair the existing system was, Jack convinced *all* of the folksingers to strike one Friday night when the streets were teeming with tourists. Faced with a major disaster, the club owners took less than an hour to agree to guarantee each of the performers a minimum of five dollars per night, plus the money in the hat that was passed around toward the end of each set. This may not seem like anything at all, but five dollars was a surefire good meal and a good start on rent. (My rent in the East Village was only fifty-six dollars a month at the time.) With three of us playing, we were now getting fifteen dollars a night to work with. More importantly, the deal was a concession to all performers that became a precedent for future arrangements. And at the time, it was something we all felt we deserved in the name of our dignity.

Jack helped many performers and their managers. He simply loved the music and used his promotional skills to help the people he enjoyed. I was one of those people and he became my first real manager—without a contract.

Another who fell under Jack's wing was Bruce Murdoch, a Canadian and a Village legend who disappeared before most of New York and the world had a chance to really hear him.

Jack discovered Bruce in Montreal and the more he told me about him, the more I was curious to see Bruce for myself. So after my first gig in Ottawa, Canada, that Jack also had arranged, we went to Montreal and I was very impressed.

Bruce was a prodigy in the purest sense of the word. He was a seventeen-year-old-singer-songwriter so brilliant and so well read that he was asked to teach a special course in literature at McGill University. Jack was right. This kid could write, sing, and play and we were both anxious to see him come to the Village as soon as he could get there. We thought Bruce was going to set the world on its ear.

So we stayed overnight to see Bruce play again. Jack was hoping to convince him to go back with us to New York, but a funny thing happened that delayed our trip for two more weeks—and also helped my career.

Without me knowing about it, Jack spent the afternoon at the two major Montreal newspapers and practically beat the music writers over the head to get them to come down and see me. Bruce was the featured performer who was already well known throughout Quebec, but when I got to the club, the manager conveniently asked me to do a guest set.

The next day one paper had a fifteen-inch story about an "angry, anti-Vietnam American folksinger" singing about social injustice. The other paper had a fifteen-inch story about the same American folksinger (me), who was "funny," "articulate," and "so easy to relate to," who "pulled no punches in a time of national [American] turmoil." They both were *me*.

I'm not sure what these reviewers were smoking that night, but each must have had a different supplier. Anyway, after those reviews, the manager of the club insisted I stay on for two more weeks and the place was packed to the rafters for twenty-eight straight shows.

So Jack brought Bruce to the city and the kid did just what we thought he would do. He knocked people out. They called him "the Canadian Bob Dylan" and he *was* a lot like Dylan; the same way Donovan was a lot like Dylan. The same attitude, the harmonica hanging from his neck, the big acoustic guitar, and songs that really meant something. Bruce had a very advanced literary knowledge and his writing was indeed special. He wrote songs about world peace, America's problems, and sophisticated songs about personal relationships. His relationships. With women.

Jack tried to get Bruce on the Newport Folk Festival when it was brought to Carnegie Hall in New York City after the franchise to produce the festival in Rhode Island had run its course. But Bruce was turned down. By George Wein, the same promoter who ran the Newport gig, who knew nothing about Bruce.

Even so, Jack managed to get Bruce a spot on the Carnegie Hall stage when Bob Gibson agreed to call Bruce up to do a single song. The next day's newspapers went out of their way to point out how good this stranger, Bruce Murdoch, was and how a new star had been born. The big question on the street was: "Who was that kid, who sang one song and brought down the house?" Bruce even did an album that year that attracted some attention as one of the best of the year. Unfortunately, that was about all we would ever really see of him.

Bruce was underage and without relatives in the United States. He had overstayed his visa and could not get an extension. Suddenly he lost all the momentum he had built up. He had to go back to Canada. He was so disappointed that he stopped singing and writing. He went to western Canada and became a lumberjack for six years or so. But Bruce did leave behind several reminders of what he was about and the atmosphere we lived in. Here's one he wrote, the one he sang at Carnegie Hall.

LET'S LAY DOWN OUR DRUM

The truth's gotten lost,
its been strangled and tossed
by the noise,
and confusion of battle,
has left it so rattled it's poison
The future must think that barbarians come
let's lay down our drum
let's lay down our drum

Soldiers mark time,
to the criminal mind,
as they pass by and our Governors smile,
'cause the Nuremberg Trials never asked why,
our homicidal police don't convict anyone
let's lay down our drum

And it's useless political talk,
that's kept everybody strung

And it's evident both sides should stop,
they already deserve to be hung.
Let's lay down our drum

Fools get upset,
without thought they forget
about reason.
And the citizen who marches,
is slandered by charges
of treason.
You know songs of this kind,
should not need to be sung,
Let's lay down our drum,
Let's lay down our drum.

Back in the Village, it was time to put my own career into a higher gear, so Jack put his fine promotional skills to work. He was a man who seemed able to figure out more shortcuts than anybody I ever met. He was the master of the shortcut. He made me believe that shortcuts really exist.

In early 1965 he gathered some newspaper clippings about a performance I gave at an NYU protest rally (to save a small park) and he used the clippings to get us a serious gig at the Night Owl Cafe. I mean, they actually paid us fifteen dollars a night. Next he printed up buttons with his own money that read: WHAT IS A RICHIE HAVENS?

Pretty soon you could see people wearing those silly buttons all over the Village. "What we're going to do next should really get you going," he said to me. "We don't need to wait for someone else to realize what's going on. We'll do it ourselves."

Jack wasn't fooling around. I was playing to packed rooms every night at the Night Owl and Jack knew it was time to take a risk. So he simply rented out Little Carnegie Hall and promoted my first real concert that *sold out* and attracted a very positive review.

My mother and father came from Brooklyn for that show. It was the first time they had seen me perform. They had never even seen me when I was in my doo-wop group—the Centurions—performing at the famed Apollo Theatre, much less playing the guitar and singing solo.

My parents were never sure about what had been going on with me after I left home. My dad had spent his whole life as a factory worker and an electroplater. But his love of music always revealed where he would have rather been—playing on some stage. He was a great piano player. Self-taught. Now he was watching his son make music on a real New York concert stage. He was in shock, but I could see how proud he was. I needed nothing more from that audience that night. Both of my parents were right there in front of me. I was okay. They knew I was okay and I could feel that they knew it. My mother stopped worrying about me, which was a relief for *both* of us.

With that concert and Jack's help, things picked up quite a bit for me. I was that much closer to recording my first album.

show business disease

Once a performer enters the public arena, he begins to face choices that have nothing to do with his art. *Trying* to become famous or rich—or both—is not what I was about, not when I started, not now.

I was fortunate to get to the Village when I did, at a time when you could say what you really felt and there were many things worth saying.

For more than six years, I had been playing the coffee-houses in the Village before I got a recording deal and that occurred only after I had practically erased the idea from my mind. Getting a record deal was a sign of success and recognition for your work. It meant that your music would be heard by thousands of people who never saw you perform in the wee hours of the morning at the Cafe Wha? But at the same time, it was a complicated issue with me. Maybe more than it needed to be. But the issues were important. They still are.

RICHIE HAVENS

In some ways, getting a record deal meant that you were selling out.

Because you had to be willing to do what the record company wanted. You were going *commercial*. You were not necessarily going to record the songs you played in your gigs. You would do songs the producer or the company executive thought were "right" for the time or the market . . . You might even have to do your music the way the record company wanted, not the way you wanted. In other words, a deal meant that you were going to face choices you never would make on your own and in those days the record company owned your publishing rights as part of the deal—if your manager didn't already.

On the positive side, you would get some new instruments and a little pocket change and if the record turned out to be a success, you would get exposure and a chance to play some good gigs and maybe in a couple of years you would get the royalties they said you earned. (Starting out, most of us would have died just to hear one of our songs played on the radio. We had no idea how they got there.)

If you were a singer-songwriter doing your own material, that was different. But even in the early 1960s there weren't many. Chuck Berry and Carl Perkins were among the first to break the mold in the 1950s, along with some doo-wop groups on small storefront record labels, but only a handful of the singer-songwriters who signed with established record companies were being given the license to do their own stuff in their own way.

Even Dylan's record company—Columbia—didn't initially let him record much of his own work. His first album, simply titled *Bob Dylan*, included mostly traditional folk songs and a couple of low-key originals. None of his searing songs of social commentary were on that album. That was very puzzling to those of us in the Village who had heard him perform in cafes. The Dylan we knew had already written dozens of songs. Some were serious, others were quite funny or contemporary parables. Even a few—the "talking blues" types—had a rapid, staccato meter that would fit right in with today's rap music. Having Albert Grossman as his manager, however, quickly changed Dylan's situation. Grossman understood the financial potential of a singer doing his own songs and when the first album was successful, he was able to negotiate the next move forward in Dylan's career. At least, that's the way it seemed to me.

From what I could see at the time, all but a few singers went into the recording studio with the understanding they were not in control of their own sounds. Choices were being made for the artist, choices that had nothing to do his or her sensibilities. Yet, in spite of these contradictions, I had no argument with the system. I understood it perfectly. It was theirs.

It was the record company's game.

It was their money.

They were the ones inviting you in, not the reverse.

Knowing this did not exactly inspire me to pursue a recording deal when I knew that someone with no real feel for my music was going to be sitting behind a desk or a glass partition telling me what sounded right and what did not. And there was always another important part to the recording experience that gave me an uncertain feeling. In fact, it was an issue that has remained at the core of so many personal decisions faced by performers in every era: How much do you want to become famous?

Fame is a Pandora's box. In some cases, it is the natural and proper accolade for doing something really well. Lindbergh's solo flight across the Atlantic, for example. Or, in music, the awe we hold for Duke Ellington's incredible body of work. Yet the prospect of fame can motivate the performer to greatness, or it can be a devilish seduction that keeps any performer from developing his or her natural talent to its ultimate levels.

And there is another, equally important side to the issue of fame. The side that many famous people complain about the most. The loss of privacy, which I believe is at least partially self-inflicted. I learned this a long time ago in the Village and so many times later while traveling the world and making numerous TV appearances.

Whenever I walk as fast as everyone else, no one notices me. But when I walk slower than everyone else, many people take notice and I can't get four blocks in forty-five minutes. You can bet several people will begin pointing me out to friends, or hand me something to sign, or gather around while I sign autographs. And I sign every time I'm asked.

I am one of those performers who enjoys direct contact

with people in all walks of life—and have shared good conversations with thousands of people in dozens of countries—but it is clear to me that people seeking extra attention get exactly that. Those who move quietly on with their lives, even in show business, usually get the privacy they need.

In other words, celebrities who do not want attention and publicity are hardly likely to show up at the glamour events, with glamorous dates, ready for the photo op. Becoming famous may not be a bargain with the Devil, but *trying to become famous* certainly is!

Some artists cope well with intense public acclaim, or they learn to accept it just to achieve a platform to reach more people. Some very famous artists and musicians are able to accept the deals they strike with record companies and publicity agents because they know they will gain the freedom to do what they want—eventually.

Look at Dylan, the Rolling Stones, the Beatles, Chuck Berry, Paul Simon, or Joni Mitchell. They did not sell their souls to the company store. All gained control over their careers as they became enormously popular. Their tremendous success *empowered* them to make most of their own artistic decisions. And this was the major change that set the record companies back twelve paces. They had to open up to managers seeking independent production deals for their performers.

But other artists, those who enjoy fame a bit too much, or crave it, or do exactly as they are told, seem to pay a steep price for it. Elvis Presley is one example that comes to mind.

Elvis was an amazing phenomenon in the late fifties,

exposing a pretty good version of black rhythm and blues to white audiences just as Chuck Berry, Little Richard, and Bo Diddley were finally gaining airtime on mainstream pop music stations with some of the greatest rock 'n' roll of all time.

Sam Phillips, the adventurous record producer and owner of Sun Records in Memphis, wanted to find a new sound and he saw considerable potential in Presley when he first walked in the door as a part-time truck driver. Presley's raw singing voice and natural electricity lit up the room.

But as I understand it, Presley's earliest attempts in the studio didn't excite anyone until Phillips relaxed his control in the sound booth and let Elvis run loose with his own musical ideas, a blend of Southern blues and rockabilly, a style that was fresh and inspired. Just listen to "Mystery Train," or "I Forgot to Remember to Forget" or his rocking version of "Blue Moon of Kentucky" or all of the original *Sun Sessions* recordings. That's pure Elvis, very early, down to basics, yet probably as good as he ever would sound.

Elvis was out on the road with some of that material without much notice until Colonel Tom Parker came into his life and took the raw Elvis step by step to superstardom. Almost overnight, Parker, who had managed country singer Eddy Arnold to considerable success, made Presley into an international superstar of the highest magnitude.

A bigger recording deal with RCA Victor . . . Nationwide television appearances . . . Movie and merchandising contracts . . . Vegas.

Elvis became one of the biggest stars of the twentieth century. And with that heady success, this young well-mannered fellow of modest means from the small town of Tupelo, Mississippi, naturally leaned on the worldly Colonel for a whole lot of advice. About everything.

As I see it, there are two kinds of performers: those who hire managers to work for them and those who think they work for their managers, or at least believe they have to satisfy them. I think Elvis fell into the second group, perhaps for good reason.

His friends say Elvis worried constantly about his standing at the top of the pop heap, even though they constantly reminded him how good he was. Instead of so much praise, Elvis probably needed a little blast of reality and it is no wonder to me that he died an unhappy man who sought relief from his pain through his pills. Elvis loved singing to people. I believe that was where he felt most comfortable.

Things happen for a reason. All things. Years later, I would get to see it in Elvis's eyes firsthand when I ran into one of his band members in Las Vegas who told me that Elvis was excited to know I was in town. I was opening for Liza Minnelli at the Riviera, invited to do so out of the blue by her musical director and drummer, Bill LaVorgna, who played on my first album.

I initially thought without a doubt that this was going to be strange, but it actually was incredible to work with her. Anyway, I ran into the band member again and was told that Elvis said hello and invited me to his dressing room before he was going to go on.

I couldn't believe it. Elvis knew who I was?

I was accompanied to Elvis's hotel and through the maze of corridors to his dressing room. When I entered, he was sitting combing his hair. He saw me in the mirror and smiled, turned, stood up and opened his arms. I felt like I knew him for my whole life. We hugged each other like we hadn't seen each other in twenty years. He was conscious of his weight and it was obvious he hated being like that. I told him I was really overwhelmed and sincerely happy to get to meet him. He said, "I feel the same way about you, man. You're too much." Then he said, "Hey, man, do me a favor . . . walk me to the stage."

Now, there was no way I could have believed that this could be happening to me, but it was.

So I walked with him, back through the snaking hotel corridors. We hugged each other again. He wiped the sweat from his brow. The door opened and a blue spotlight crashed into the corridor. He was a silhouette for an instant and was gone. The doors closed and I walked back through the casino hallway and went to my dressing room at the Riviera remembering the look in his eyes. He was desperately trying to be who he was. A really nice and ordinary guy.

Elvis was not the only casualty to fame, not the only one to die essentially of what I call "show business disease," a disease that is as real as cancer if allowed to take root. Every one of the famous performers we have seen die of drugs or other excesses was taken by this same show business disease, a disease of isolation and/or no privacy. Every one of them.

Janis Joplin was so lonely on the road that she drank and used drugs to excess. What a voice! What a soulful moan, what a longing for love. What a tragedy. The minute she was made to give up her adopted family—Big Brother and the Holding Company—and had to work with the band that Albert put together, Janis felt lost. She died of a broken heart caused by the business. Leaving her band behind left her with a hole in her heart and haunting, insecure thoughts.

Jim Morrison was another who died of show business disease. Here was a guy who wanted most of all to be a writer. He rebelled at every turn against being trapped into the mold of a rock 'n' roller to be groped and gawked at. Yet at many of his concerts, Morrison literally threw himself into the crowd; let people maul and manhandle him; cursed wildly at the authorities; whipped the people around him into a blind frenzy as if he was totally unconscious of his power. At times, he was. Bombed out of his brain. In complete escape from the world that wouldn't let him be himself.

In the end, Jim seemed *that* close to finding a private space in France, where he was being encouraged to write poetry, to draw, but it was half-past the hour of his reckoning. As I said, all Morrison ever wanted was to be a serious writer, a poet, a filmmaker. He died lonely and confused, with too many drugs in his system.

Jimi Hendrix?

I knew him well. In fact, I sent him to the Village.

I had just released my first album when two guys from Paris opened a place called the Cheetah, a hot night spot on

Broadway and 52nd Street that was rivaling the Peppermint Lounge and Arthur's for its fifteen minutes of notoriety. It was, in fact, the largest discothèque in New York with live music. At the time, I had several friends that I jammed with, playing completely different music than I was performing in the Village clubs—and we managed to get a two-week gig there to open the club.

When the two weeks were finished, I decided to go back to the club to party and mingle and I was so early I felt embarrassed. So I stood at the 100-foot bar with forty other early birds. We looked like five people at that huge bar. Suddenly Wilt "the Stilt" Chamberlain was standing next to me. I'm six-foot-two and my eyes were only level with his chest. It blew my mind. I said hello and we began a conversation. The policy at the Cheetah was continuous live music. One band would end their set with a song the next band would walk on and also play, allowing the first band to leave the stage without stopping the music.

There was a band playing—*Not bad,* I thought—when suddenly I noticed that the guitar playing was unusual and that wasn't all. This guitar player had the instrument upside down and somehow was clipping the strings with his *teeth,* or his *tongue.*

I couldn't believe my eyes or my ears. The sounds and licks were way out there. Was he really playing the thing with his *teeth????* I found myself crossing the empty dance floor that could easily have held 2,500 dancing people.

I moved closer to the stage, bent way down low, and

looked up, trying see what he was doing. He actually was play-ing lead guitar with his teeth.

No trick. There was no tape recorder off to the side playing his licks. *Far out!*

A few tunes later and I knew this was not a circus act, this was quite simply the greatest guitar player I had ever seen. Amazing range. Lightning speed. Pure notes. Two melodic lines at once.

U-n-b-e-l-i-e-v-a-b-l-e. When they left the stage, I felt, be-cause I had opened the club for the previous two weeks, I could go backstage without a problem and he blew me away by telling me he had played with Little Richard before coming to the city from Florida through the musicians' union.

I told him he should not be the backup in *any* group, that he didn't need to be playing for Little Richard or anybody else. He was good enough to be out front with his own group. He was the best guitarist I'd ever seen.

He asked where things were happening in the city and after he told me he was staying uptown, I told him to get down to the Village. That's where he could find many young musicians looking to play. Right then and there, I decided to hook him up with Manny Roth at the Cafe Wha? Within a month, Jimi put together his first band: Jimi James and the Blue Flame.

Jimi might have been totally unknown to the general pub-lic at that time, but he played to packed Village crowds of teenagers night after night and some of the most famous rock 'n' roll guitarists in the world went through major changes whenever they stopped to see him play. Especially the few I sent down to the Wha?

A music-loving lawyer friend of mine, Johanan Vigoda, brought members of the Yardbirds and the Kinks and their manager over to see me at the Night Owl. They were flipped out about how I used my thumb, but I said, "No, no, you haven't seen anything. Come with me." And I took them around the corner and into the Cafe Wha?

They came away so visibly shaken and depressed from Jimi's awesome, powerful performance that you could tell he had made these skilled musicians see that he was in another league way above anything any of us ever thought to reach for.

I shook my head watching their expressions as Hendrix did his thing from song to song, from riff to riff, from behind his back to his teeth. It was mind-boggling how he blew some of the finest guitarists in the world completely away.

In Chicago two years earlier, I had met Paul Butterfield and his guitarist Mike Bloomfield and I was excited when they came to town to play at the Cafe Au Go Go, where I was like a permanent opening act. I didn't have time to stay with him, but I brought Mike over to the Wha? to see Jimi. Bloomfield never did make it back that night for his opening set and when he did show up, he was very depressed.

He missed his opening set. On opening night.

The next morning I found him at the Cafe Borgia, staring through cigarette smoke. "I'll never play the guitar ever again," Bloomfield said. "I just saw the best string bender I've ever seen in my life."

Bloomfield did play, of course, even better. In the end, he was inspired by Jimi.

A few years later—after Woodstock, in fact, at the Isle of Wight Festival in the British Isles in late August 1970—I saw Jimi Hendrix again. He was now a huge success, recognized for his genius, praised universally, just as Bloomfield had praised him, "the best guitarist in the world." But he was terribly unhappy, extremely depressed, and he asked for my help.

"I'm having a real bad time with my managers and lawyers," Jimi said. "They're killing me; everything is wired against me and it's getting so bad I can't eat or sleep . . . You've been doing this longer than me, man, I need to talk to a lawyer, man. You must know somebody."

I told him I had a very good lawyer he should talk to— Johanan Vigoda—a legend in the music world and a man who was going to play an important role in my recording career. I told Jimi I would be glad to introduce him and that I would be in London for four days after the festival and would be going directly back to New York. I told him to come by and see me when he left the Isle of Wight.

Jimi never showed up.

The next thing I heard about him was some three weeks later. He was found dead, a drug overdose. Another great, great talent trying desperately to do his thing, a truly unique human being who found the pressures and the competing influences around him too much to bear. The truth is, he didn't actually die from an overdose of addictive drugs as was first reported in typical scandalous fashion by the press. He died from being up for days at the festival, drinking a lot of beer and not being able to sleep. He took sleeping pills, threw up in his sleep, and choked to death.

Another victim of show business disease.

I do not believe I am exaggerating when I say that all of these extraordinary talents turned to drugs, alcohol, and other stuff as escape from the ordeals and routines of high-powered show business. Perhaps it is easy for people to label such abuse as self-inflicted excess, but I have seen some of my best friends go under from very close range and I know how painful it was for them to endure another deadly symptom of show business disease: the isolation and the loneliness in the midst of the madding crowd.

Performers with the rarest of gifts—like Elvis, Jimi Hendrix, or Janis Joplin—got tons of praise or scorn for things that fell real short of their real talents, things that did not deserve such attention. They were pampered to the point where they lost *real* time and sense of themselves.

That kind of adulation is hard to stop while it is happening. Sadly, people who surround the victims of show business disease usually are not much help. In fact, most performers find themselves relying too much on the people who made them stars. This does little for their need to get a true sense of themselves, much less to grow or live happily.

The simple truth is that decisions made by managers or advisers are only designed to keep their performers' careers on track, not to help the performer enjoy freedom, or live more responsibly. Their primary goal is to make a percentage of what the artist makes, without whom they would not have a job in what they call "show business."

Fame is more than a goal; it is a way of life and it can be a seductive trap that few people are prepared to handle.

Those that do handle the trappings of fame may shine in the limelight and make contributions to the world that go beyond their artistic talents. Muhammad Ali is a great example. So were Arthur Ashe and John Lennon. Such people are very rare. True inspiration is an aspect of life so little understood by those who shuffle the papers.

In my case, I had no delusions of grandeur. I didn't care about becoming rich or famous. Not then, not now. My goal was to communicate, to do only the music I loved.

12

mixed bag

I n the mid-1960s, I was all for finding new ways to express myself. Recording my music certainly was something I wanted to do. In the back of my mind, I knew something would come along when it was right. And I believed that no compromise would be necessary. At all.

Enter Jerry Schoenbaum. Jerry was quite successful and highly respected when he created a new label from the dormant Verve record label and the defunct Folkways label at MGM records in 1967. He called it Verve Folkways. Jerry had been president of several record companies, but he got tired being the guy doing all the work for somebody else. Every time he made a barrel of money, "the Board" would tell him to make three barrels more. With Verve Folkways, Jerry saw the chance to start his own label from scratch and he decided to use the forum to promote a few Village artists he had wanted to record that the big companies were afraid to: Janis Ian, Tim Hardin, the Blues Project, and me.

The four of us became the backbone of this resurrected label. MGM left Jerry alone and he gave them hundreds of thousands of sellable albums that they distributed from coast to coast.

Janis Ian's "Society's Child," written when she was thirteen, was a powerful hit on the folk and pop music charts and it challenged radio stations everywhere because of its daring lyrics. Tim Hardin's "Reason to Believe" and "If I Were a Carpenter" sold well enough, but more importantly introduced other singers outside the Village to Tim's classic songwriting. Although most people don't know it, the *publishing* end of the music business can be far more lucrative than the *recording* end and Jerry was one of the few record company execs who was into helping the artists he signed.

Formed by Al Kooper and Danny Kalb, the Blues Project took its name from a low-profile album of the same name that featured a collection of blues tracks by Dave Van Ronk, Geoff Muldaur, Eric Von Schmidt, and Kalb. Way ahead of its time in many ways, the project sold their share of recordings, but were even more popular as a live act on the cutting edge of the serious musician-based rock 'n' roll bands that would rise to prominence in the mid 1960s, to the present day. Bands built around Eric Clapton, Jimi Hendrix, Peter Townshend, Stevie Ray Vaughan, and other virtuoso guitar players.

The Blues Project went through several changes in personnel during a brief life span, but the first album with Verve Folkways was a live gig with guitarist Kalb, drummer Roy Blumenfeld, bass player-flutist Andy Kulberg, guitarist-vocalist

Steve Katz, singer Tommy Flanders, and the piano-playing Kooper, who had already spent a few years with Dylan during the mid-1960s and played that classic organ riff in "Like a Rolling Stone." The Blues Project was well named. It was quite a project for Jerry to keep so many diverse styles together, but while they survived they played great folk blues with a jazz accent. And they rocked.

Jerry and I got together because he knew that Albert and I were not satisfied with my first demo recordings. Albert tried several times to record me with different-style musicians—jazz guys, rock bands, even country musicians. So finally he decided to dump the project on to his partner John Court. This was now 1967 and almost five years after I signed with Albert when he first came to town.

John Court was exactly what I needed. Here was a talented producer, a serious professional with an open mind who actually understood that I had a lot of ideas about how to interpret a song. Even though I played acoustic guitar, we both agreed that I was not really a pure, traditional folksinger.

"I think we should avoid an album of pure folk songs, or rock 'n' roll songs, or songs of any one type," he told me. "Not because I want to tell you what to do or how to do it, but because that is not what you do onstage.

"You sing ballads, Richie, *and* you sing folk songs, *and* blues, *and* jazz," John said.

"You have a deep, resonant voice that carries a lot of emotional range . . . You probably could sing opera if you wanted . . . So let's bring the real you into the studio along with a few musicians who work in jazz, blues, rock 'n' roll, *and* folk. Why don't we let you do what you do? A *mixed bag*." At the time, John had a few ditties of his own he was working on and one came from a riff in a Bill Evans song that he wrote the words to. I thought it was great and asked if I could do it. John was delighted, but said, "Maybe the next album."

Mixed Bag had "Eleanor Rigby," a great Beatles song about isolation and loneliness; "Just Like a Woman," an insightful, sensuous Dylan song; "San Francisco Bay Blues," a folksy-skiffle tune that I slowed down and changed into a bluesy love ballad; the Judy Henske song "High Flying Bird," written by Billy Ed Wheeler; "Follow," a beautifully written, philosophical tone poem by Jerry Merrick that became a signature to my performances in the years before Woodstock; "Sandy," a quiet, almost jazzy ballad that had movie theme quality, and "Handsome Johnny," a searing antiwar anthem written by Lou Gossett, Jr.

Yes, *that* Lou Gossett.

I had known Lou since my early poetry-reading days in the Village. Before I even started to draw portraits. And I saw him awkwardly perform several folk tunes and work songs in some hootenannies onstage throughout the early sixties. But I had no idea he was an actor until one day Deano and I saw him on the screen in the classic *A Raisin in the Sun*.

I was sitting in a Village movie theater, staring up at a ten-foot version of this man who looked very familiar, when I realized it was the same Lou I knew from hanging out at the Cafe Wha? Apparently, Lou wanted to sing and play the instrument a whole lot better than he did at the time, so, while in Chicago working on the flick, Lou practiced and practiced. After a year on the set with *Raisin,* he was back playing the guitar—onstage—as if he had been studying for years.

One day Lou said he had written a song about the absurdity of war. It was during the Johnson years—the Vietnam War years—and most of us strongly felt that our country was making a terrible mistake playing anything but a peacemaking role in that civil war between North and South Vietnam.

Most of us were heartsick and angry about the fact that hundreds of thousands of young Americans—including a disproportionate number of black men and other minorities—were being sent ten thousand miles to fight a brutal ground war against a people who never threatened us. For me this was the second time—after the Korean War. The antiwar feeling most of us had wasn't against the country we lived in, or the historic role America supposedly played to help defenseless nations remain or become free. The Vietnam War was not a war staked out on such high moral ground. It was a war in which our leaders invented incidents to justify an increasing military presence, a war *against* our own stated principles of freedom and fair play.

Few people may remember, but long before President Kennedy sent "observers" into Vietnam as military advisers to the South Vietnamese government and long before President Johnson gained war-making powers after the highly disputed Tonkin Gulf incident, there had been a democratic election in South Vienam won by North Vietnam's Ho Chi Minh. That may not have been the result we wanted to see at the ballot box, but it was the result we were pledged to honor. Unfortunately, the United States completely ignored the outcome because Ho Chi Minh was a Communist.

That notwithstanding, most of us in the Village felt our songs of protest were expressing our patriotic duty. We wanted world peace. We were stating clearly that the government that was elected to represent the American people was not in Southeast Asia for any good reason we could believe in, much less for the people living there. We began to have to accept that the people who were *representing* the American people no longer *reflected* the American people. They were instead pushing forward with their own agendas and secrets.

Lou's song "Handsome Johnny" was a great antiwar song, a song about *all* wars to which I added a few verses and would play at Woodstock. Calling it a "protest song" or an "antiwar song" probably was accurate, but whenever we call a song a "protest song" or attach any such labels to any artistic endeavor, we have to be careful. We just may be limiting the potential audience to people who already believe in the artist's point of view. Lucky for me, my audience was way above such narrow typecasting. And I found out when I played "Handsome Johnny" in my first of more than a dozen appearances on *The Tonight Show*—a year before Woodstock—that those who were to discover that I even existed, were typecast, even by me.

The live audience was mostly made up of visiting tourists

from the Midwest. I thought they might not like "Handsome Johnny" because it spoke sharply about the war we were in. To my surprise, the audience understood perfectly what was being said about war in general. They stood and applauded until Johnny Carson went to commercials, and they stood and applauded through the commercial break. They were *still* applauding just as enthusiastically when we came back on the air. The moment was unmistakably powerful.

Most people watching at home had no idea that the applause never stopped, but Johnny saw firsthand what was happening and spontaneously walked over to where I was standing and invited me back to perform again the next night and to do another song right then and there. Later he told me that the only other performer he ever invited to play on consecutive nights was Barbra Streisand. But she had another concert and could not make it back.

HANDSOME JOHNNY

Hey, look yonder,
tell me what's that you see
Marching to the fields of Concord,
It looks like Handsome Johnny
with a musket in his hand,
Marching to the Concord war,
Hey, marching to the Concord war.

THEY CAN'T HIDE US ANYMORE

Hey, look yonder,
tell me what you see
Marching to the fields of Gettysburg,
It looks like Handsome Johnny
with a flintlock in his hand,
Marching to the Gettysburg war,
Hey, marching to the Gettysburg war.

Hey, look yonder, tell me what's that you see
Marching to the fields of Dunkirk.
It looks like Handsome Johnny with a carbine in his hand,
Marching to the Dunkirk war,
Hey, marching to the Dunkirk war.

Hey, look yonder, tell me what you see
Marching to the fields of Korea.
It looks like Handsome Johnny with an M1 in his hand,
Marching to the Korean War,
Hey, marching to the Korean war.

Hey, look yonder, tell me what you see
Marching to the fields of Viet Nam.
It looks like Handsome Johnny with a M15
Marching to the Viet Nam war,
Hey, marching to the Viet Nam war.

Hey, look yonder, tell me what you see
Marching to the fields of Birmingham.

It looks like Handsome Johnny with his hand rolled in a fist,
Marching to the Birmingham war,
Hey, marching to the Birmingham war.

Interlude:
Hey, it's a long hard road,
It's a long, hard road,
It's a long, hard road,
Before we'll be free.

Hey, what's the use of singing this song,
Some of you are not even listening
Tell me what it is we've got to do
Wait for our fields to start glistening
Wait for the bullets to start whistling.
Here comes a hydrogen bomb.
Here comes a guided missile.
Here comes a hydrogen bomb
I can almost hear its whistle.

In the early eighties I added another verse to "Handsome Johnny." Sadly, new verses almost add themselves.

Hey, look yonder,
tell me what's that you see
Looks like he's tryin' it some more
Here comes Handsome Johnny
and he's tryin' it again

But we didn't let him get down to
El Salvador.

It took all of four days to make *Mixed Bag* and I'm glad people still respond to the songs when I play them in concert. I know I still find fresh musical ideas in many of them and the technical quality of the original recording is a tribute to John Court's openness. He was a new breed of producer who became very good at his craft and we were on the same page every step of the way. He produced my next album as well, *Something Else Again*, which did have that song he wrote on it: It was called "Sugar Plums."

like a small earthquake

Things had been going well for me by the summer of 1969 . . . I had already played the Newport Folk Festival and was booked for hundreds of gigs in America, Canada, and Europe. I had two albums doing well and a third on the way.

Woodstock was an idea that had been brewing since the Monterey Pop Festival on the West Coast in 1967. All summer, we were hearing on the streets of the Village that a big East Coast festival was going to happen, but we weren't sure where. There were plenty of stops and starts, a lot of disappointments, all of which the press wrote about.

Large numbers of people were hanging out, camping out in the town of Woodstock, then Wallkill, waiting for the final details to be worked out. So when all the court challenges and injunctions and complaints ran their course and the Aquarian Music and Arts Fair at Woodstock was moved forty-five miles away in late July to Max Yasgur's 600 acres on a hillside in Bethel, New York, thousands of people picked up their sleeping bags, parked their vans, and trekked down the road to the promised land. Thousands upon thousands were also coming from just about every state in this nation.

Today it was finally happening. For real.

Our helicopter landed right behind the stage. There was a farmhouse with a big front yard that was covered by cars. Once I got out, I looked around and saw three roads on or near the farm. All were blocked by the blanket of people, especially the road on the bottom of the hill that went to the staging area. There was no dressing room. The only place to change clothes or get tuned up was in the farmhouse or under the stage itself, which was eighteen feet off the ground, a huge structure with extremely tall sound towers alongside and out in the field. The lights seemed to be in place, but they were still finishing the stage. *Far out.*

I was impressed. It was an awesome scene and quite mellow everywhere I looked. Even the people nearest the stage weren't clamoring for anything to happen. It was a summer day and they were having a good time in the country. Some were smokin' pot, dancing to portable radios, or throwing Frisbees around. Some were lying in the sun or taking naps or making out under blankets. But most of all they were meeting and hanging out with each other. No matter where they came from or how old or young they were.

The vibes were good on this spot. So good you can still feel them to this day when you go there. It still feels the same

The marker commemorating the original Woodstock festival.
(*Daily News L.P. Photo*)

to me. It's a wonderful place. But now it was getting late and I knew something had to happen soon. I went under the stage and saw Tim Hardin playing his guitar, singing a little to himself, just trying to stay as relaxed as possible. Tim, as I said earlier, was a great talent, a very sensitive songwriter with an unusual voice. (He even liked the chords I used at a time when I couldn't even tell him what they were.) But Tim also had a serious drug habit. He was delicate like glass and everybody knew it.

We had a brief conversation about nothing I can remember and I went back over to the spot Deano and Daniel had staked out behind the stage. My bass player, Eric Oxendine, was missing. He'd decided to come up on his own and we were sitting there saying, "He's not gonna make it." I thought, *I know he's not gonna make it . . . he's not crazy enough to walk the fifteen or twenty miles from the spot where traffic was stopped.*

A few minutes after three o'clock, the organizers approached Tim and asked him if he would go on first. We were about fifty yards away and I could hear him say loud and clear, "ARE YOU OUT OF YOUR *MIND*? ARE YOU C-R-A-Z-Y OR WHAT, MAN? I'M NOT GOING OUT THERE FIRST. NO WAY, MAN. ABSOLUTELY NOT! FORGET ABOUT IT."

I didn't blame him. But then they came to me.

"Jeez-us, Michael, not *me.*" I said, half-laughing, half feeling like I was being told to go to the dentist. "There's no way you're getting *me* up there. Nobody's throwing beer cans at *me* just 'cause you're three or four hours late. They're not killing *me*, man."

That was the first time they asked me. Michael Lang didn't press the point because he said he had another band coming in by helicopter. Soon. But the bubble helicopter only brought in half the band—It's a Beautiful Day—and the pilot was starting to see the big picture.

"I'm out of here," he said, throwing up his hands. "Y'can't expect me to ferry over a hundred musicians three at a time with all their equipment; not in this thing. I'm outta here."

They at least convinced him to go back for the other half of It's a Beautiful Day's band and he took off back to the hotel driveway.

By this time, the organizers and county officials felt they had only one way to hold the situation together. So many people . . . this had not happened before to anyone.

"What the hell do we do?"

"Only one choice. Call in the *National Guard*. Quick."

The Guard was not called to round up people or to stop the pot smoking—because the truth was, those who were toking out there were severely outnumbered by those who weren't—by at least 800 to 1, maybe 1,000 to 1. The ones that were doing grass generally sat together in groups, which played into the illusion. There certainly were no riots in the crowd. The truth is, there was no trouble at all. But even so, without the Guard there would have been no festival, or very little music and who knows what else, especially in the rain on the second day. The National Guard actually came to *save Woodstock,* and that's something kids today really should know. Besides, they were part of the experience we were all having.

So many of us were against the Vietnam War—or war *any-where* in the world. We weren't against the people in uniform. Why would we be against them? They were our brothers and cousins, uncles and fathers, here and in Vietnam. Besides, *they* didn't start the war.

It was the soldiers who transported all the bands and the amps to the stage; it was the soldiers who brought in plenty of food and water during the weekend. A lot of them probably would have been sitting down in the crowd if they didn't have to be in uniform. We knew we were lucky to have *our* soldiers there when we needed them and they needed a break.

Another forty-five minutes passed and I started to get edgy. Somebody had to get up onstage soon, just to hold the fort. The organizers must have had the same thought, 'cause here was Michael walking slowly toward me and I knew exactly what he was going to say. I could see his great smile getting larger and larger as he came closer . . . then he cocked his head to one side and said, "Richie, please help us out. Oh, man, you've *gotta* help us out."

When I realized he was serious this time, I could feel my heart start to freak out. And I was pleading with Michael. I said, "Michael, I'm supposed to be *number five*, not *one.*"

"Please, Richie, man, *pleeeeese,*" he said.

I was finally convinced. But I replied, "If they throw one beer can at me, you're going to owe me—big time."

I was only stalling a little for time. I knew what the situation was. I calmed myself with the thought that it would only be a twenty-minute set. I picked up my guitar and climbed the steps. The crowd went nuts. I felt the people just wanted something to happen after all the hours of nothing.

So I sat down on the stool and looked out at the huge crowd and said what I had been thinking since that first look from the helicopter at the never-ending blanket of people.

"YOU KNOW, WE'VE FINALLY MADE IT," I said into the mike. "WE DID IT THIS TIME. THEY'LL NEVER BE ABLE TO HIDE US AGAIN."

The rumbling roar from the crowd was like a small earthquake. It came first in a low-pitched wave, then it rose up and shook the stage. I heard the word *freedom* loud and clear in my brain. A word I would hear over and over again while I was up there. I was home, among long-lost and newfound friends.

We were there because we felt good about ourselves, happy to be in the same place with so many brothers and sisters who shared this unspoken common bond. We were there to look at each other, meet each other, identify our support for each other. We were there to celebrate. We would share this experience the rest of our lives.

There were smiling faces in every direction and plenty of people over fifty in the crowd. Huge numbers of college kids, of course, but I had no trouble seeing plenty of parents and grandparents with their families—adults who believed in world peace like we did and wanted to hear the music we played. For some reason, this too was omitted from most press accounts. We were all rebels forced into a cause who learned along the way that we had plenty to embrace. We had ourselves. We had the good sense to prefer peace, not war. We were not down on America. We were Americans with the highest ideals. And we could see all around us that there were way too many of us now to be ignored.

I didn't know that being first onstage was going to be anything but a horror. Who knew what to expect? But there I was—in full view of hundreds of thousands of people. So what choice did I have but to start talking and singing? Suddenly I was in any other place I've ever been, no fear, just doing what I do. I understood who they were and they understood who I was and we were off.

That's how it works for me. I don't have a "set list," never do. Whatever happens between the first song and the last, happens between me and every audience. I know the first song I want to sing sometimes a few seconds before it comes out or while I'm tuning up and I know the last song. How to get on and off the stage. But things don't always go in that direction. Here, on this stage out in the open air, with such a staggering number of people out there, I was just living through what I do and enjoying it and sharing my music.

I was in Bethel and I was first onstage.

I began with a relatively unknown song, "Minstrel from Gault." It talks about how a minstrel in biblical times came down from the provinces with tales to tell: some false, some true. It was close to a pure folk song and it felt like an easy way to get things rolling for me. I sang more of my songs, about forty minutes' worth, which was twice as long as I expected. But I figured if they weren't pulling me off the stage after forty, nobody else must be ready yet.

RICHIE HAVENS

Which is exactly what I found out as soon as I saw Michael at the back of the stage on my way off.

"Please go back on, Richie. Do three more songs. *Please.* We have somebody coming. They're just not here yet. Sing three more songs. They're on their way."

So I went back and sang three more songs and then I looked over at Michael and his people. They were asking me to do another. So the set went on.

I didn't mind. It was wonderful. I was with my friends— my constituency—and we were a minion of many millions, including those who couldn't get there but wanted to. I left the stage six times.

Seven times in all and nearly three hours after I'd first looked out on the crowd, I'm back out there one more time, when finally I've completely run out of songs and know I've got to get off, no matter what the situation is. So I start tuning and retuning, hoping to remember a song I've missed, when I hear that word in my head again, that word I kept hearing while I looked over the crowd in my first moments onstage.

The word was: *freedom.*

And I say to the crowd: "Freedom *is what we're all talking about getting. It's what we're looking for . . . I think* this *is it."*

I start strumming my guitar and the word *freedom* comes out of my mouth as "FREE-dom, FREE-dom" with a rhythm of its own. My foot takes over and drives my guitar into a faster, more powerful rhythm. I don't know where this is going, but it feels right and somehow I find myself blending it in to an old song—"Sometimes I Feel Like a Motherless

Child"—a great spiritual my grandmother used to sing to me as a hymn when I was growing up in Brooklyn. It's a beautiful song, a song I hadn't played in six or seven years.

FREE-dom, FREE-dom, FREE-DOM, FREEDOM;
FREE-dom, FREE-dom, FREE-DOM, FREEDOM;

SOME-TIMES I FEEL . . . like a MOTH-ER-LESS CHI-LD;
SOME-TIMES I FEEL . . . like a MOTH-ER-LESS CHILD;
SOME-TIMES
I FEEL
LIKE A MOTH-ER-LESS CHILD
. . . A LONG WAY FROM HOME.

The rhythm is strong and my foot is driving me when another phrase comes into in my head that was part of a song with the McCrae Gospel Singers in Brooklyn: *"There's a telephone in my bosom and I can call Him from my heart."*

It's a phrase that seems connected to this motherless child I'm singing about. The two ideas flow together while I'm playing and my foot is driving my guitar with all the rhythm in my bones.

Deano and Daniel are following along, getting into it, chanting phrases back at me. But "FREE-dom" is always there like an unspoken bass line or distant refrain. This was the same feeling I'd been experiencing all along. The feeling that Bethel was such a special place, a moment when we all felt we were at the exact center of true freedom.

RICHIE HAVENS

Sometimes the music can pick you up and take you away, like it did to me during "Freedom." (*Photo by Mauren Brodbeck*)

I'm singing it, "FREE-dom, FREE-dom," picking up the rhythm another beat and the pulse of it is carrying me and connecting the whole Woodstock Festival for me in my very last moments onstage. It felt like I could feel the people I couldn't even see on the other side of the hill . . . "Clap your *hands! Clap your hands!"* And they all did!

People started to stand and the wave of them rising went over the hill.

I'll never forget it.

I played while walking off, away from the microphones; I played while singing across the ramp, leaving the rest of my band still on the stage. I played all the way across the road before I finally stopped. I had nothing else to sing; this song made itself up on the stage. And then, out of the corner of my eye, I could see Eric Oxendine, my bass player, walking the final few yards just as we were going off. *He did walk the twenty miles,* I thought. *He was late, but he got here!*

That last song turned out to be an anthem for me and for a lot of other people too.

We are all motherless children in some sense of the way life is. That is an equal, harder side to freedom: a sense of *aloneness,* a sense of the vastness of our individual opportunity to do just about anything in the universe. We all feel that burning need to inhale freedom. And when we taste it, we know we need to touch others who feel it too. We know it in our bosom as a basic cornerstone to human life. And no matter how many times I sing this song—no matter where—I still feel the true spirit of the so-called "Woodstock experience" and what happened there and continues to happen even today.

I stayed on the grounds for several more hours, talking to people, catching the music, taking in the whole scene, getting some rest. I don't think I ever played so many songs at one time. I was pretty tired, but pretty high from the experience, the energy all around me. It was getting dark and It's a Beautiful Day had played their set, along with a few other bands.

More bands were coming in by military helicopter and the National Guard was helping out. After a shaky start and a lot of worries, the festival was moving along great.

I wanted to stay and catch more music, but we were booked at Indiana University the next night. What happened next I will never forget. There's no doubt it captured the essence of this event better than anything.

It was on the Army helicopter transport, heading back to the hotel when I saw it. The first thing I noticed was that this helicopter was much larger than the bubble we came in. The door was like a big bay window without any glass. Exactly the kind of helicopter the troops jump out of. It was huge.

It probably had seen its share of bodies and severely injured. It probably had been to 'Nam.

It's a Beautiful Day was on board, along with my band and another band. We were all in it with room to spare. The seats were opposite each other, backs to the wall. A long bench on one side and a long bench on the other.

THEY CAN'T HIDE US ANYMORE

So I'm sitting there, facing the open door, leaning a bit on my guitar, holding it between my legs, on my lap, bracing my arms around it, staring straight out the door into the evening sunlight, seeing only the treetops, when a thought came to mind that stopped me in my tracks.

This is what it must feel like to be in 'Nam, I thought to myself. *You can't see anything below the treetops except the machine gun rounds flying up at you. Imagine what that's like. You're nineteen or twenty years old. They've shipped you ten thousand miles from Kansas or Brooklyn and you're sitting there in your uniform too scared to breathe and tracer bullets are whizzing by.*

Suddenly I could see the whole scene as if it were really happening. And to this day, I sometimes get a flash of it— back there with those imaginary tracer bullets coming out of the treetops past the open bay door . . . Here I am at this Woodstock thing, with peace, love, and music in the air, going back to the hotel in a Vietnam army helicopter. Man, that felt weird, but it was only half of it.

Slowly I turned to look down the line to the three guys across the way on either side of the open door. I turned again to look down the line on my side and saw four or five guys sitting to my right, while my own guys and another two were sitting to my left.

Most of them were guitarists and bass players. All—and I mean *all*—were holding their instruments the same way I was. They were leaning on them like they were rifles, holding them upright on their laps, between their thighs with the guitar necks straight up in the air.

The image is burned in my brain. All of them sitting there like they could easily have been in uniform on the way to another skirmish with the Vietcong. But I had to laugh at what I saw. I knew what I was really seeing was exactly what Woodstock was all about: "We're the new army," I said aloud. "We're the *new army*!"

The sign of it was right in front of me: We looked like an army. There were tie-died shirts with big splashes of green—almost like camouflage—and we were holding our *"guitar-rifles"* straight up in the air in the military manner.

As long as I live, I'll never forget that image and there's no question that I was right. We had no weapons; we had no harm in our hearts. We were musicians and singers and songwriters and we had come to Bethel from everywhere to rally the spirit and the harmony of so many voices, including our own. *We* were the new army; the new army was *us*, the new army was *all of us who were there*.

Leaving the next morning, we did not know how we would make it to the airport in Newark, New Jersey, to get to our gig in Indianapolis that night. Our driver, John Fisher, said the only thing we could do is head over to the New York State Thruway and see. We did. And we got right on without any trouble at all. The reports we heard on the radio said the Quickway (Route 17) and the Thruway were both closed because of thirty miles of incoming traffic parked on them. Not true. Only the northbound lanes were closed. As we drove along the Thruway, we waved at thirty miles of partying people who had been unable to move their cars. Traveling south, we did not see one other moving car on either side of the road all the way to Jersey. Not one. We were all alone on the busiest road in North America. Surreal.

CHAPTER 14

to make and interpret songs

People ask me what's the best way to write a song. So I tell them how *I* do it, not how TO DO IT. To me songwriting is a lot like religion. There is no one way to see God, no one way to be in perfect harmony with the cosmos. There isn't even a *best way* to do that.

There is you and the cosmos. You are in it, part of it. You are born with all the insight man has gained through thousands of years of developing the human mind, body, and spirit. The great artistic minds that have preceded us have contributed to our genes and our intuitive abilities to reach beyond what we know. Read the Old and New Testament, the Talmud, the Koran, and the teachings of Buddha and you surely will see just how much insight into the human condition was known thousands of years ago. Our inheritance.

Songwriting is no different than other creative ways to gain access to that insight. It is not something we can control as much as listen to. And it has been with us since the first Homo sapiens uttered a rhythmic pattern of grunts in caves.

The same is basically true for poetry, sculpture, playwriting, drawing, painting, photography, scientific discovery, and invention. All of these forms of expression came into being as we gained more tools. And they come to us now in elusive threads. There simply is no formula to do anything "creative." Yet, at the same time, I do write my songs in one of two ways.

- I hear a *title* rattling around inside my head and I instantly know that there is a song there. In fact, I can usually visualize exactly what the song is about just by hearing the title. The title is my window into the song.

From there I sit down and write lyrics on my computer, or with pen and pad, or even on a napkin in a restaurant if that's where I am. At the very least, I write down the title that came to me so clearly and a few ideas that I associate with it. And if I'm not as absent-minded as usual (it's an Aquarian trait), I pick up on the idea sometime later.

Once my lyrics are written, or while I put them together, I pick up my guitar to work out the rest.

- I also write songs by first hearing a compelling *chord progression*. When this happens, I know it is a song. Instantly. And I know I have to do something with it right away or I might lose it. So I either hum the new melody a few times to myself to commit it to memory or reach for my guitar to play with it over and over until I hear another, connecting melodic phrase and another after that.

Often I will play this progression for hours and hours, sometimes days, simply for the joy of its sound and to really experience the music in it, the music that will tell me what the words are. I listen and they come. It's a wonderful feeling to connect to music this way. Music tells you what the words are if you spend time and listen.

For me a good song has to have several things going for it. The musical attitude has to fit perfectly with the lyrical attitude and the lyrics have to go beyond a catchy phrase or a pretty tribute of love and affection. Being pretty or cute doesn't make it for me. I left that behind in doo-wop music and in the bubblegum records the labels were selling to my younger sister.

The first song I heard from the Beatles was "I Want to Hold Your Hand," a catchy tune for sure. I heard it from two rooms away and it stopped me in my tracks. A voice in my head said: *Finally. Something new.*

The Beatles sounded very familiar, yet fresh at the same time. Something very different. I could hear it right away, but I really didn't get into them until *Rubber Soul* came out in 1965. Songs like "Michelle" and "In My Life" were on that album and I realized the depth of original music coming from them. I don't have to tell you that every album they put out after they got their foot in the door had songs that will live forever. That is what separates popular music from truly great songs. The truly great songs are essentially timeless, even if they are about things that have happened in a specific time and place.

Listen to Dylan's "The Lonesome Death of Hattie Carroll" or "Oxford Town" and you will see exactly what I mean. Both were about specific events, terrible events that explained more about racial prejudice and the injustices of our time than most law books or newspaper and magazine accounts.

Here's a gentle yet poignant song written by Lotus Weinstock (aka Maury Hayden) that has no time and place of reference. Just a feeling shared.

CAUTIOUSLY

Cautiously you handed her a rose
Yes you did
Yes you did.

Pretending to know all a lover knows
Yes you did
Yes you did.

She wore that rose pretending that she knew
the reasons for that rose
as it grew.

Cautiously you said to her
please be your bride
Yes you did
Yes you did.

Pretending to believe that you could abide
Yes you did
Yes you did.

She wore that pretense wanting so to share
the reasons for that rose,
though dead, she wears.

Sometimes the melodies I hear do not lead me to new songs. Some develop into new ways to interpret old lyrics, including songs that were good songs when they were written and performed completely differently. Even so, I can sense that a new melody or chord structure or tempo will make a song more interesting, maybe bringing it closer to the author's original sense of emotion. A good example of that is "San Francisco Bay Blues," Everytime I heard it sung, it was uptempo and out of character for the lyric. I thought to myself, *You don't sing a sad blues song like a happy dance tune.* I thought the writer could not have intended it that way. So I slowed it down like the blues it was—lyrically—and that's the way I sang it and recorded it on *Mixed Bag.* It was the way I thought the writer originally intended it.

Much to my surprise, I found a recording by the writer

Jesse Fuller four years later and believe it or not, he sang it the same fast way everybody else did. Go figure.

And here is a song I wrote when I heard the title:

"What More Can I Say, John?"

The title came to me while I was in Canada after listening to the songs Bruce Murdoch was playing, songs that addressed issues going on in America more than most of the songs I was hearing back home. Listening to Bruce altered my perspective, opened my thinking, and expanded my songwriting . . . That's what a good piece of art does; that's what is behind the song-writing process for anyone. Giving new perspectives in your own way.

I wrote the song in my hotel room. It was like a letter to John F. Kennedy.

WHAT MORE CAN I SAY, JOHN?

You have anticipated all the players
your silent judgement growin'
And from time to time you pace the floor
because you are a knowin'
Yet you can not stop your sowin'
all the stars that symbolize where your goin';
And your heavy rains keep growin'
Hey, come on, you've got something better to do.

You have hidden your face from the people,
and to them you keep on denyin'

That far, far away across the sea,
for no reason their sons are dyin'
while it's Viet Nam your buyin'
among all your conservatives a-sighin'
and all your murderous lyin'.
Hey, it's me who's defyin'
Hey, come on, you've got something better to do.

What good are all those documents?
those well-kept worthless scrolls;
When the hand you bit turns and slaps your face,
the hands you tried to mold,
And they leave you out in the cold,
with your pockets full of gold,
Yet you cannot pay the toll,
of the brave and the bold who are shoutin'
Hey, come on, you've got something better to do.

People make a big mistake when they think making music is something only a few people can do. Making music is a perfect, completely natural form of human communication. ALL people—and I do mean *all* people—have the capacity to hear *new* music in their heads and to express it in an infinite number of ways. Those of us who stop to do something with the sounds or musical ideas we hear (or stumble upon) are just paying attention. There is nothing more to it and nothing less. Just get a pen and pad when a line comes and write it down.

Maybe it will tempt you to finish it. Maybe it's a song that I will end up singing someday.

The part I hear most vividly when I hear a song is the melody and that is where I begin, yet there are many songs with beautiful melodies that don't have lyrics that match their beauty or their emotion. Every once in a while, however, a truly inspired song comes along that does. These are songs the writer allows to come through them and not from them.

I feel that songs like that are universal in their nature and serve a higher purpose, something people will recognize the world over. They tend to relieve us of the tensions we are imprisoned by. They tend to lift some part of the weight we seem to be carrying or clarify the path we are taking.

How many times do we hear music in a movie that accentuates the emotions we are witnessing in the characters or the plot itself. The songs that I have chosen to sing are indeed songs that have done that for me.

Sometimes I hear a song that shines, even though the singer may not have a great voice, but it is the interpretation that puts it across. A song like "Morning, Morning," which was on *Mixed Bag,* comes to mind. A really beautiful song that matched its melody, as originally done by the Fugs. When I first heard that song, it was clear there was something very special in its message and its melody.

This may sound strange, but I have always thought that I was capable of hearing the intent of the writers or the singers that sing such special songs. For me, Bob Dylan always was *the best interpreter of his own songs* and all I did was invest my energy and my voice into what I felt was his emotional intent.

Sometimes very popular songs actually become obscured by the limitations of those who get to record them first. Some years later, someone will come along to rerecord such a song and reinterpret it. All of a sudden the song that was always there is heard more acutely and more people get to appreciate the original effort. When I listen to a song, I want to appreciate what the writer or interpreter felt when they were under the influence of a song's magic.

Being able to write and sing your own songs is a privilege to be cherished. To be able to affect people who can hear or feel what you are saying between the lines is to truly communicate the whole message in the song. That, after all, is what songs are really about . . . messages.

It is a weird feeling to hear some of my friends talk about today's music as if it is so different from what they claim to be *their music*. Many of them feel there is nothing going on anymore, their golden age is over, never to be experienced again. But they do not appreciate how they grew up with their music and now everything they enjoy—as far as they are concerned—is nothing new. What they don't see is that *everything is new*.

When I first started, folk music was an acquired taste and assumed to be too "culty" for distribution to a wide audience. At least the record companies were very slow to appreciate the general appeal of such music, and as far as I'm concerned, they still fail to see the potential worldwide audience. And it is a simple ironic fact that the folksinger-songwriters of the 1960s had such an impact on popular culture that it turned the music business upside down, changing it forever, opening the door for hundreds of hit songs that had serious lyrics, lyrics with deep meaning.

Today every musical genre is filled with poignant messages. Every song is a folk song or a song about the folk now experiencing personal battles of progress (or nonprogress). Many of my friends forget that their music served their own needs in their time, just as today's young people are being served by making their own music. Don't we remember when our parents and grandparents could not make heads or tails out of what we young people were doing or trying to say?

Didn't our music grow from our need to fight through the system to say what we needed to say? Today everyone can do that. Through the generations we mark time and savor the memories of special experiences with the songs we made possible. We remember just where we were when we heard a certain song and what we were doing.

When people grow or make big leaps in their art, they are bound to leave some people behind. It's the natural order of things. This is what Dylan did when he publicly plugged in his electric guitar for the first time—at the 1965 Newport Folk Festival. I was there to see it. I was in the audience, sitting next to Albert Grossman, who managed us both.

I knew Dylan was going out onstage with a band for the first time, because they had rehearsed in the same house I was staying at in Newport. I thought it was great. *Wow, yeah, this is it,* I thought, watching them. *Now he's really going to rock and sell some records to people who never listened to him before.*

I thought immediately that he was broadening his reach. But the fact that he was doing it in a so-called traditional folk festival did contribute to an "in-your-face" atmosphere. To tell you the truth, when they tuned up and began to play, I thought it was kind of loud. But that was not Dylan, that was the soundman. The volume was up way too high. By the time they brought the decibel level down to normal, there already were plenty of people reacting to him: booing.

I felt for him. I saw right into his eyes and he looked confused, bothered by the reaction. I felt a sinking feeling in my stomach for him. I felt a loss, almost like death. A loss of his opportunity to move ahead.

I thought they were rejecting him without even listening, not giving him a chance. Oh, he went through with his set and it sounded good to me. And Peter Yarrow told the crowd that he would be coming back, and he did, to play a very well-received acoustic set, even borrowing a mouth harp from the audience. But I was left with a definite feeling that a break had occurred. Dylan was moving on without his folk audience and into another world. I thought about it while he was playing and after he finished and realized how important the moment was and how he was being unfairly placed in a jacket by people who had been so antiestablishment. Ironically, they were only stuck in their own traditions.

He wrote the songs he was singing. Wasn't he entitled to his view of how they should be performed?

Time provided plenty of answers to those who doubted that Dylan knew what he was trying to do all along. Always a mysterious character, Dylan was wonderful from the first moment he came on the scene. He was Zorro. His songs chronicled the stories of our times and he wrote timeless conceptual poetry, songs that included everyone, even though they seemed to be about someone specific. His songs always included many perspectives and points of view.

In "Ballad of a Thin Man," he challenges Mr. Jones: "And you don't know what it is, do you, Mr. Jones." *All* of the anonymous Mr. Joneses—from media reporters to politicians to not-so-innocent-bystanders of life—are included somewhere in the song . . . In "Mr. Tambourine Man" and "Like a Rolling Stone," whole bunches of different people and their perspectives are represented. He was saying things that anyone could identify with: It's not just me or one of us out here, *everybody* is out here.

In many of his songs, one line has nothing to do with the previous line. Each line connects poetically but is its own whole story. There was some great magic in Dylan. And people have yet to realize, even those who continue to buy his records, that for a long time, he was one of the greatest guitar players in the world. Every song had its own rhythmic pattern, never two alike, and almost impossible to copy. Like my own individual style of guitar playing, Dylan didn't think about what he wanted to play, he just played. But unlike my playing, Dylan really knew what he was doing where I only knew that I didn't know.

For a long time, I've been calling rock 'n' roll the first generational primal scream. The voice of an entire generation, which started in America and made possible like-minded communications that crossed over great bodies of water and distant time barriers for the first time in the history of mankind. (Nothing new, huh?) . . . Jazz may have had that potential, but it was mostly instrumental, while our music was built on lyrics, addressing ideas of real life and changing the whole world. The feedback now comes to us in the music and art of today's adventurous minds from every neighborhood, culture, and country.

None of this comes in a vacuum. We are all influenced by what is happening on our radios and in the clubs and movies we watch and listen to. I know I was fortunate to live and learn so much in the Village, where so many great performers regularly interpreted their unique songs and those of other songwriters. Among them all, the one who affected me the most when I was forming my voice, my sense of interpretation, was Nina Simone.

A Juilliard-trained student and one of the finest piano players in the world, Nina found it difficult to find work in the orchestras with which she was trained to play. So she added her voice to her magnificent playing and became one of the most insightful interpreters of songs written by others, as well as one of our greatest contemporary songwriters.

It was Nina Simone's music that I heard on the radio in the 1950s that instilled deep within me the idea that it was okay to do what I found myself doing in the 1960s. The songs that I would choose to sing were songs that affected me greatly as a human being. And I have to admit that the way I played the guitar had a great deal to do with the way I sang those songs.

In 1963, after playing in the Village for little more than a year, I not only had the pleasure of accompanying a singer by the name of Steve DePass on a tour sponsored by the Ford Motor Company, but also to see and hear Nina Simone, who was on the same tour.

The promoter had a keen idea that he could put together a caravan show that would travel in station wagons and vans (Ford, of course), first to Washington, D.C., for ten days at the Howard Theatre and then to ten universities on the East Coast. I cannot tell you how incredibly wonderful it was to be able to stand side-stage and watch my idol play three shows a day along with other great stars of that time.

Among them were Herbie Mann's orchestra, Mongo Santamaria's orchestra, and Willie Bobo's band. I was scheduled only to play guitar for Steve DePass, the emcee of the show who also sang a few songs each night. On the seventh day at the Howard Theatre, the woman who took care of Nina's wardrobe told me that Nina wanted to speak to me. I didn't quite believe her, but she convinced me it was true and also told me to bring my guitar. Well, I grabbed my guitar and headed for her dressing room on the other side of the stage. When I entered, totally nervous, she was sitting at a dressing table, putting on her makeup. She looked at me and nodded to me to sit down and then asked me if I knew the song "Sinner

Man." Not only did I know this song, I had learned it from her record.

I apologized to her, though, for not being able to play the guitar in the normal way. Without skipping a beat, she said, "I don't play the damn piano correctly either."

I think she said that to make me feel comfortable; she knew I was very nervous. "Play the damn song," she said. So I picked up my guitar and played "Sinner Man" the way I had done onstage back in the Village. About halfway through the song, she said, "Okay that's fine. One of these nights I will call you up to play it with me."

I couldn't believe my ears. *Me? Playing with Nina Simone?* Oddly enough, for the next three days she said not one word to me. I was completely baffled, but I didn't question the situation. It was not until we made our first university stop on the tour—St. John's College in Annapolis, Maryland—that something happened. First of all, Willie Bobo's band left the show and an incredible folk group took their place: the Modern Folk Quartet, which happened to be four friends of mine from the Village. After being out of town for ten days, I was so happy to see people I knew that I went backstage to visit with them while Nina was on. It was the first time I was not side-stage for her show.

Suddenly Steve DePass ran in to the dressing room and interrupted us, telling me that Nina was calling me to the stage. I could hear her playing and singing, so I said, "But she's out there playing now. I can hear her piano. How can she be calling me?"

"Just get your guitar, Richie," Steve replied. "She's calling you. Right now!"

Okay, I thought. *Maybe she said something before she started singing.* So I grabbed my guitar and headed for the stage. When I got closer to the stage, I finally heard what she was singing. She was playing a sort of Bach fugue and singing the words:

"*Rich*-ard, where *are* you.
Please get *your guit-ar*
and come to the *sta-age*"

over and over again.

I couldn't believe my ears, but that didn't stop me from running out there, grabbing a stool, and dragging it straight to the piano. As soon as I sat down next to her, she broke into "Sinner Man" and we both went wild. The audience completely freaked out with applause and that was the origin of the first public review I received. For the next four days, we did "Sinner Man" together right in the middle of her show, just her and me.

The next thing I know, I am invited to her hotel room to practice a song that Miriam Makeba had written for her, which I also got to play in the middle of her set for the next two days. All of this is such a vivid memory for me, partly because of what happened three days before the end of the tour.

We were driving along to the next university and had to stop for gas. We had been telling jokes and laughing like hell: Mongo, another master conga drummer we called Potato,

Nina, her husband, and me. As we pulled in to the gas station—still laughing at one of Mongo's jokes—I could hear a
voice on the radio coming through the gas station doorway. I
wasn't sure but thought I heard the news commentator say,
"The President has been shot with a machine gun." (For those
who don't remember, those were the first news reports.) I then
asked Nina to turn on the radio in the car, that I thought they
said the President had been shot. Well, they started laughing.
They thought I was telling another joke and it took a few
minutes to convince them to turn the radio on. The news was
on every station and the car became very solemn. When we
got to the next hotel, we did what everybody else in America
did that day. We ran to turn on our TVs to find out what had
happened. It was simply one of the saddest moments in my
life and of course the tour was over. From that moment on,
there was a new depth in everything I sang or interpreted.

stormy forest

During the recording of my third album—the last of three I was then under contract to do—I was called to the MGM Building for some publicity meetings for *1983*, a double album due to come out in late 1969. Even though Verve was a subsidiary of MGM, this was the first time I'd even been in the building. The MGM Building.

Albert had told me my contract was ending with Verve Forecast and that the parent company, MGM, was renegotiating with him. But if they called me, I should not commit to anything. Albert also told me that he was trying to get $10,000 as an advance for my next recording, which was twice what I had gotten for the first two. While in the MGM Building, however, I had to stop by the promotion director's office. After some friendly conversation, he told me that Albert had been there the day before and was offered $15,000 for me to do another record.

He then said that I should think about asking for my own label.

"My own label? Are you *sure*?" I didn't think I was in that kind of position and wondered if I really could do something like that. "With a working budget?"

"Absolutely, Richie," he said. "You're making them a lot of money. Your first two albums sold more than a million copies and they don't want you to go to another label. Trust me," he said. "It's there for you if you want it."

I guess you could say that the offer directly led to my decision to break away from Grossman, who disappointed me a great deal when we had the following conversation the next day.

ME: The promotional guy said that MGM would give me my own record label.

ALBERT: They're just playing with you, Richie. No way they're going to give you your own label.

ME: I don't know, the publicity guy seemed pretty sure that it was a done deal if I just went in and told them what I wanted.

ALBERT: No way, Richie. But, I did get *ten thousand dollars* for you for your next record. That's twice what they gave you for the first and second one.

I didn't speak for about ten seconds. I just looked at Albert and realized that we had to end our relationship. I didn't tell him that I knew they had offered $15,000. Privately, I was pretty upset that he would tell me one thing and it would turn out to be something else.

For the better part of the next week, I talked with Johanan Vigoda about the label idea and realized it would be smart to let him do it for me. He was someone I had come to know personally during my earliest days in the Village. Among other things, he happened to be *the* most respected contract lawyer in the music business.

Johanan asked me what I wanted to do. I said, "Record my own albums and record other artists that the *big guys* wouldn't record because of the messages in their music." Much like Jerry Schoenbaum's Verve labels opened the door for me.

"How many?" he asked.

"At least four," I said.

"Want an office in the building?" he asked.

"Yes," I said, getting a bit frightened at the prospect.

"You'll need a phone, a secretary—and your partner and road manager to get a salary, yes?"

Mark Roth, my "partner and road manager," had written songs with me, photographed my album covers, coordinated travel for gigs, and was going to coproduce my next album with me. He also became my partner in Stormy Forest Productions.

"Yes," I said.

"Okay, Richie, I'll put the package together. We'll talk tomorrow."

The next day Johanan called to tell me MGM definitely was interested in talking.

My deal turned out to be worth more than $650,000 and I got everything I asked for. I imagine this was very embarrassing to Albert, but it certainly was best for me. I already had signed with the William Morris Agency and was signing thirty contracts a week for gigs. I was booked eighteen months in advance at mostly colleges and universities all over America.

"I think I'll go my own way from here," I told Albert. "Thanks for everything." While he was alive, I never let him know that I knew he had deceived me and at least we remained friends, nothing heavy. He couldn't believe I actually pulled it off, but I did. The label was called Stormy Forest Records and I would record most of my albums on it.

Johanan was brilliant for sure and quite a character too. Once he practically laughed when he saw me and some jamming buddies doing yoga exercises in my house, but then he wanted to know what possible benefit could come from anyone standing on his head.

I explained how yoga helps cleanse the body by reversing the circulation in the capillaries. With that brief explanation alone, Johanan became a passionate devotee to the practice. It took him months to do it, leaning against the wall. He would even stand on his head in executive offices while negotiating heavy deals and invite everybody in the room to join him. What a sight that was. They all thought he was nuts, but they always called him first when they needed the best.

One time I was in Johanan's office while he was on the phone, talking long-distance, when he ate through two or three pencils, plus a few pieces of paper on his desk. He was a very nervous type who always needed to do something with his hands or mouth. He also was a Capricorn (the Goat).

Finally he said, "Wait a minute, I can't seem to find where I put the contract. Let me look for it. Wait a minute."

Then he realized he had chewed through the contract papers he was looking for.

About two years later, I was in Cannes for a World Music Publishing conference when I overheard some producer types and lawyers at the next table and one of them said with a French accent, "And he *ate* the contract."

They all burst out laughing.

I turned to these people and stopped them all cold, saying, "Johanan Vigoda. Right?"

The Frenchman's mouth nearly dropped to the floor.

"Yes, yes, Johanan. But how do you know about that?"

"I was there," I told them, "I was in the office when he ate the contract while he was on the phone."

None of this should fool you or anyone else about Johanan Vigoda. He has been a legend in the music business for thirty years. He's probably responsible for so many of the best ways to set up music contracts that there are few lawyers in the trade who do not call upon him first for advice when they have a sticky problem. He is the lawyer's lawyer in the field.

And he also knows his music and art. Johanan was responsible for introducing the Japanese film director Akira Kurosawa (*Ran* and *The Seven Samurai*) to America, as well as the Brazilian jazz singer Astrud Gilberto ("The Girl from Ipanema") and her musician husband, Joao.

For years, Johanan had been asking if he could do anything for me and there never had been a chance to take him up on it. When the time presented itself, Johanan came through in royal fashion.

My deal with MGM opened up a new world for me. I had an office on the twentieth floor and a generous budget to produce my albums. My partner Mark Roth, who had photographed the Beatles and many of the early album covers on the folk scene, was put on the payroll and I was able to hire an old friend from Brooklyn, Bernice Wise, as my secretary. MGM had three floors of offices and studios in this midtown Manhattan building on 55th and Sixth Avenue. The company distributed records for the many different labels they created, but most of these labels were destined to lose money over the next few years. Most, but not mine or Casablanca Records, which had Spanky and Our Gang.

My label, Stormy Forest, was the natural extension of Stormy Forest Productions, the production and publishing company I started while I was doing my third album for Jerry Schoenbaum's label, which evolved into Verve Forecast under MGM. This was a double album with sixteen songs, titled *Richard P. Havens, 1983.*

It had some great songs on it, including Maury Hayden's "Cautiously"; a pair of Lennon-McCartney classics, "Strawberry Fields Forever" and "She's Leaving Home"; a rarely played Dylan tune, "I Pity the Poor Immigrant"; and several of my own songs. The year was 1969, the year that would be Woodstock, and the title of *1983* was based on the idea that

I thought we already were in the world created in George Orwell's classic novel *1984* that warned about the dangers of a monolithic society. My album said there was "still time, brother," but not much.

Being Albert Grossman's partner, John Court was out of the picture, so Mark and I produced *1983* ourselves. Producing albums meant I could put together all the sounds and arrangements I heard in my head and control the quality of the product that would be sold to the public.

My first album on Stormy Forest was called *Stonehenge*, a title I had carried with me since an earlier trip to England when Mark and I saw the ancient, mysterious Stonehenge structures. We crawled around in the fields after closing hours near sunset and Mark took photographs, some with the sun peeking through the main Stonehenge rock formations. We knew immediately that one of Mark's photographs would be on the cover of my next album.

For *Stonehenge*, we used my regular guys: Eric Oxendine on bass, Natoga (Daniel Ben Zebulon) on congas, Deano (Paul Williams) on guitar, guitarist Monte Dunn, and Bill LaVorgna, one of the finest drummers in the world. Bill, the only musical director Judy Garland ever had (and later, the musical director for Judy's daughter, Liza Minnelli), was a personal friend who would play on my next album too.

Stonehenge was recorded in about nine days, with little time for sleep or fooling around. We practically lived in the studio and went at it with great passion and got the music down that we wanted. There were songs I had written with Mark, songs by a few friends, and songs of my own . . ."Open Our Eyes" and "Prayer" were two very special songs on that album.

"Open Our Eyes" was a song that had stuck in my brain since I was a teenager in Brooklyn. It was a gospel song I remembered hearing many times on the radio, the first song I was able to do from my youth. It felt great to do it because it belonged and I didn't have to ask anybody what they thought. It was my label. My choice. The song told us that if we open our eyes we can see that we really have all we need right in front of us.

On "Prayer," I wrote and sang all eight voices a capella. It was a song of perspectives, a song that was a toast to all who see the outside from within or see the inside from without.

PRAYER

To all those outside the inner side
Let not your heart be heavy
There are those who understand
It is not easy
. . . It is not easy to tell a lie

To all those inside the outer side
Let not your head be heavy
There are those who understand
It is not easy
. . . It is not easy to know what to do

And to all those who understand
Let not your words be heavy
There is he who understands
It is not easy
. . . It is not easy to be a mother and a father

There were forty separate labels under MGM when Stormy Forest was born. Even when we were starting out, there were signs that the company was looking to close out many of the other labels for a possible sale. Still, this was a great opportunity for me to do my own thing and the bottom line was just as clear: If we made good albums that sold well, we would be helping them too.

Stonehenge was a good album that sold very well. So did *Alarm Clock*, which we recorded with Bill LaVorgna, Eric Oxendine, Deano, Natoga, and a piano player named Alan Hand.

Alarm Clock was just as the title suggested. A warning. It also was one of the few times I have used a song's title to name one of my albums. *Alarm Clock* was being made in the context of the Vietnam War that was still raging. Four students protesting the war had been shot dead in May 1970 on the Kent State University campus in Ohio. Large crowds were gathering in many cities, pleading for the end to America's involvement, but the administration did not care about anything the public seemed to feel. The war would go on, regardless of public sentiment. We were seeing our government step way over bounds. *Alarm Clock* felt like a warning to awaken. The song's lyrics are as follows:

ALARM CLOCK

The Alarm Clock
. . . On the wall
and no one sees
. . . it at all.

You go have a pleasant dream
. . . and try to find out what it means
as the hands, yeah, yeah
point your way home.
The Alarm Clock
. . . calls us all
to see just what's behind that wall.
You try to read those signs while
I go look for better times
as we all
. . . make our way home.

The darkness lights the way
as the clock runs out another day
You . . . may have nightmares now
wait until you see how
we all pay
. . . back the loan.

The Alarm Clock's striking one
and you think you're having fun.

The Alarm Clock's striking two
. . . brother, you think you know what to do
. . . The Alarm Clock is striking three
you hope
. . . you know who to see.

Everybody, it's striking four
and you're pounding down another door
. . . Striking five
is there any one here alive
(Six!)
We're halfway home
. . . we're halfway home
. . . we're halfway home.
The Alarm Clock moves the time
. . . and sends us
. . . out to find
. . . the rhyme
. . . We know all the words
and don't know just what we've heard
as we all go crawling home,
crawling home,
crawling home.

Alarm Clock also had several other good songs: "Younger Men Grow Older," "Missing Train," and "End of the Seasons," which I wrote with Frank Sinatra in mind. I thought it might be a good song for him to sing before his retirement. Little did I know he would sing for another twenty years. Now I might use this song when my day comes.

The song stemmed from a piece of classical music written by Bob Margoleff, a recording engineer who had one of the first Moog synthesizers in the city. This was the same synthesizer Stevie Wonder would use to record every song on *Music of My Mind*, an outstanding album on which he played every instrument.

Margoleff's piece was a beautiful rondo (a classical form with repeating phrases) and he gave it to me as a gift for Christmas. While listening to it, a new song emerged in my head. The words and music for "End of the Seasons" just came out so naturally. The song was built around the four seasons as an allegory for the seasons of a full life. Frank Sinatra came to mind repeatedly as someone who had been living just such a life.

Here are the final two verses from "End of the Seasons":

In autumn days when it was clear
I watched the coastlines
from the mountains
in the west wind.
Down below the sea would call me
and I would find
the beaches dark and lonely
but I could see
. . . the starlight.

Darkness shore comes early
Yet it moves so slowly
like a shadow
on the hillside.
Etched in snow
I leave the doorway
Satisfied
to hear the north wind cry
. . . and it cries
. . . Winter . . . Winter
Hmmmmmm . . .

We released a single from *Alarm Clock*, "Here Comes the Sun," that did so well it made the charts for several weeks. That was my favorite Beatles song for quite a while and still is one of the happiest, most hopeful songs I sing. It played an important role in the scope of the album because it is such a youthful song, a song of pure hope. The sun is coming up every day. That's the real story. It's going to be all right. Everything works out. Everything changes. Everything gets to the point where the smile comes back. Even in the loneliest of winters, here comes the sun, here it comes. I think "Here Comes the Sun" also showed George Harrison to be a fine songwriter in his own right, working as he did under the shadow of two giants, Lennon and McCartney.

"the clock on the wall"

I met John Lennon and Paul McCartney through John Fisher, the limousine driver who took my band to Newark Airport on that surreal drive the morning after my appearance at Woodstock.

John Fisher was one of the people who had a lot of reasons to hate Woodstock, having lost his limousine business in the Woodstock mud. The huge crowds and thousands of abandoned cars near the festival site left him with just one of the several limos and fourteen station wagons he leased to ferry performers in and out. We were to be his only passengers. Once he took us out of there, there would be no way back for the rest of the weekend. The major highways were closed going north and the rains only made things worse. For two weeks after the event was over, John was unable to get his cars out of the mud and back to their proper owners. He lost everything in the deal.

John was very philosophical about his situation and had about as much fun as anybody who was there. The friendship we formed remains strong to this day. In fact, John made friends with lots of people through the years, including John Lennon.

A month after the Woodstock Festival, Mark Roth and I were still talking about what had happened in Bethel. Although we knew they wouldn't let it happen again, we both believed there was enormous potential in similar music festivals and we further believed that they could be carried live to the world, via pay-per-view telecasts in movie theaters, the same way heavyweight boxing matches were being telecast. Taking it another step further, we envisioned a complete worldwide festival, featuring the best local bands—live on the theater stage—added to the telecast of top-class international groups.

We knew that to pull off a theater-TV event would require lots of money and we knew it would never come from the *suits* in the business. It had to come from someone or some group sympathetic to our causes, preferably people who also were into the music. Both of us immediately knew who we were thinking about: the Beatles.

By strange coincidence, or great karma, Mark got a phone call the very next day from his ex-editor at *Life* magazine, who now was the chief editor of a new business magazine, *Fortune*. Mark was asked if he would do a shoot of two businessmen from England who were coming to New York to promote their new record company. At first, Mark was turned off by the idea of shooting a couple of rich businessmen—until he asked the editor for more information: "Oh, it's these two young guys from a company called Apple, Apple Records, I think."

Mark almost jumped out of his skin . . . He was going to photograph Paul McCartney and John Lennon? Proud owners of Apple Records? Unreal!

"I know I can't be there with you, Mark, but if they give you any chance to ask them about our idea, you've got to do it," I said. "What a huge break this is."

So I left Mark's house feeling pretty good and was heading to my apartment in the East Village when I noticed that the Salvation Club on 4th Street had Jimi Hendrix and the Chambers Brothers playing. That was too much good music for me to pass up.

When I got to the entrance, the doorman said to me, "Hey, man, my brother is coming down in a little while and he'd love to say hello to you." I did not know him so I had no idea who he was talking about. Inside, I watched the Chambers Brothers from way in the back and talked to Jimi for a while. Then I moved to another section behind a glass partition on the side, where only a couple of girls were sitting and there was plenty of elbow room.

I was just sitting there when three men came out of the dark around the glass toward me. I couldn't believe my eyes when I recognized two of them. John Lennon and Paul McCartney were heading right toward my table. They sat down right across from me.

I was totally speechless, but I was howling with laughter inside, thinking: *I can't wait to tell Mark that I met them before he did. I can't wait to bust his balloons that I met them first!* Mark, bless his heart, could be pretty cocky at times.

"Hi, Richie," the third man said and now I recognized him as John Fisher. John Fisher was the doorman's brother and he was driving John and Paul around New York.

So here I was, sitting on one side of this table with John Lennon and Paul McCartney facing me, telling me over and over how much they loved what I did with "Eleanor Rigby" while my tongue was completely tied to my tonsils. This went on for several minutes until a young woman got up from her table, came around the glass partition, and stood right next to Paul to ask him a question that obviously had been bothering her awhile.

"Is it true you wrote 'Lady Madonna' about America?" she asked.

As she said it, I went through the words in my mind and thought, *Wow, I never thought about that before. And you know, there just might be something that heavy in it.*

But Paul's answer revealed something about himself that made me see the Beatles a lot more clearly than any of the things written about them at the time. (Including all the psychedelic interpretations everybody seemed to be putting on their songs.)

"No. As a matter of fact, it is not about America at all," Paul said. "I was reading *National Geographic* magazine when I saw a photo of an African woman with her baby and the caption said 'Mountain Madonna' and I said, 'She looks like a "Lady Madonna." ' That's really what started the song for me."

Normal guys, I thought to myself. *What comes to them comes through them, no hidden messages, no fake mysteries to mess up our minds.* It cleared up the whole picture for me.

Even so, I never did ask them about my idea for a world-wide festival (and neither did Mark when he did his photo shoot with them a few days later). All I could do was sit there silently, taking in the experience as a tongue-tied fan. Yet, I did see their warmth and intelligence and even the whimsy in John Lennon's eyes. We saw each other many times after that and in his final months I believe he had a strong premonition that something was going to happen to him. I know I did.

I heard it on his final album in a song he wrote. It was not the first time something like that happened to me. It actually hurts to talk about it.

Sometime during the summer of 1980, I called John to find out if he had any new songs that I might be able to record and was told he was in the studio, working. "That's great," I said. "Don't bother him. I'll catch him in a few months. Don't even tell him I called." I couldn't wait to hear what he was going to do. It had been years between albums from him.

In late November I was in California for two weeks of gigs and was picked up at the airport by Gary Green, a good friend. Gary had a van complete with a terrific sound system and he always had the latest albums set up and ready to play for me on the way to his house. I looked forward to those rides.

"I've got the new Lennon album, the one he did with Yoko: *Double Fantasy,*" Gary said.

"Man, that's great . . . I've been waiting to hear it." I didn't know Yoko was on it until Gary mentioned it, so I asked to hear her side first.

Gary cued the album on the cassette player and was struck by the quality of Yoko's stuff. There were good songs, more interesting music than I had heard from her before. But I couldn't listen to John's music. The first verse of the first song Gary put on troubled me. I got a bad feeling from it right away. It sounded like John knew something was going to happen to him . . . He was singing about watching wheels go round . . . and having to let it go.

Four or five lines later, I knew I didn't want to hear any more. I had already heard too much. "Please turn it off, Gary," I said. "I can't listen to it."

Gary was taken aback, but he stopped the tape and looked at me in silence. I told him the story I'm telling you now. It traces all the way back to my Brooklyn days when I heard a disc jockey on the radio say: "Here's the last song ever recorded by the great Johnny Ace: 'The Clock on the Wall.'" (The B-side was called "Forever My Darling.")

The lyrics to "The Clock on the Wall" sounded as though Johnny Ace was marking time while something bad was going to happen to him. At least, that's what I heard in the song. And a few years later, I had the same gut reaction while listening to Chuck Willis's "Hang Up My Rock 'n' Roll Shoes." A lot of people thought this was a happy-sounding song, but it gave me a depressed feeling when I heard it was his last single, just before he died.

The same thing happened to me in 1964 when I heard

Sam Cooke sing "A Change Is Gonna Come" (while the B-side lamented, "Brother, Where Are You?"), just weeks before he died. And it happened again in 1967 when I heard that Otis Redding died after recording his classic hit "(Sittin' on) The Dock of the Bay." All of these songs gave me a bad feeling about what was—or had been—happening in the lives of these great performers. The songs depressed me. They were so different than the usual material each of them did.

So after doing my gigs in California, while Gary was driving me to the airport for my flight back to New York, the whole eerie feeling about these songs came full circle. A disc jockey on the radio said, "Here's the last song done by Elvis Presley: 'The Clock on the Wall.'" I looked at Gary and shuddered. I felt like an earthquake was going to happen right in the car. It was the same song Johnny Ace did before he died. The same song that started all of this for me. Gary began to understand.

Back in New York, I wasn't in town a day when a disc jockey at a club where my friend John Fisher was working asked me out of the blue, "I'll bet you can't tell me what Chuck Willis's last song was."

When I quickly replied, " 'Hang Up My Rock 'n' Roll Shoes,'" it surprised him enough to ask me how I could possibly know that. So I ended up telling the story again, including the strange feeling I now was living with about not wanting to listen to John Lennon's "Watching the Wheels" (a song I have not yet listened to, although from what I heard it may have been one of his best).

The group I was with thought I was nuts, but I had been carrying this dreaded feeling with me now for weeks and the question only brought it to the surface all over again.

John Fisher and I left the deejay's apartment together, but before we split to go our separate ways on the corner of Central Park West and 74th Street, I reached into my gadget bag and turned on my miniature portable TV, when the news announcer said, "Today is December 7, Pearl Harbor Day." I turned to John as he was walking away and said, "Watch your back today, John, it's *sneak attack day.*"

It was shortly past dawn and I walked all the way down to my office on 52nd Street. It felt good to get some air and not to have to think about what was forcing itself into my mind. An hour after I arrived, I got a phone call inviting me to a New York screening of *Stir Crazy*, a film with Richard Pryor, with whom I worked on another film, *Greased Lightning*.

Richard was going to be there. It was shortly after he burned himself and I was hoping to see how he was doing. We had very little time to talk before the premiere, but he was fine. He escorted Patti LaBelle, another friend I knew growing up in Brooklyn. But he left the theater early when a fight broke out in the balcony. *Man, the guy can't even see his own movie because some jerks are busting things up,* I thought to myself. Anyway, everybody in the theater was invited to go to a special impromptu dinner at Tavern on the Green, a great restaurant in the middle of Central Park. They supplied buses for everybody, but I walked over.

I was sitting there with Sidney Poitier, Harry Belafonte, and the entire cast, getting ready to eat dinner, when I spotted Peter Yarrow in a tuxedo, walking in the door. I had never seen Peter in a monkey suit before and he came right over to me and whispered in my ear, "John Lennon just got *shot.*"

I groaned and jumped up at the same time and headed for the door, when Peter stopped me again and said, "It was some guy from Hawaii." And I immediately thought about the connection to Pearl Harbor.

It was right after midnight on December 8, the day after the anniversary of the 1941 sneak attack. And later we would learn that the supposedly unbalanced killer was carrying an album he wanted John to sign, but somehow turned his mission into a sneak attack of his own. (He was also married to a Japanese woman.) It was all too much like the Japanese envoy waiting with papers for President Roosevelt to look at. While his country was bombing Pearl, they walked in and arrested him.

Lennon had been shot in front of his apartment and it felt like Kennedy all over again. But this time it was really personal. John Lennon was flesh and blood and spirit, a man who continues to remain alive through all he left behind, including his friends. One of his friends was John Fisher. Lennon liked and trusted John so much that he employed him to take care of his yellow Rolls-Royce when he and Yoko were deported for two years. The Rolls was given to the Smithsonian, but Lennon eventually gave John the original registration as a token of their friendship.

meeting michael sandlofer

S ome people go through life making a major difference in everything they do. Such a man is Michael Sandlofer, a man in love with the deep blue sea and all that swims within it, a man who believes in the intuitive goodness of children and precious few adults. In 1974 I met Michael under very unusual circumstances and the meeting led to an unbelievable series of adventures involving things about the sea I never dreamed I'd know.

A very close friend of mine was getting divorced and was pretty bummed out. His money was gone and he desperately wanted to go to Europe for a clean break to get his head straight. Somehow he convinced me to buy his houseboat, which was docked on 79th street in New York City in the West Side Marina.

A houseboat?

What was I going to do with a houseboat? I'd never been

on anything more than the Staten Island Ferry and a few fishing boats in my life.

I was making good money doing all kinds of gigs, so I went along with the deal, more to help my friend than to suddenly become Captain Nemo. After a week or so, I went down to the marina to see exactly what I had gotten myself into.

"Holy smoke, this is a real *house.*"

I was pretty surprised how comfortable I felt sitting inside this forty-foot floating home, complete with three rooms, a small kitchen, work space, a bathroom, and communications equipment.

I looked around and listened and felt like I had completely left the city. No cars. No noise. Just the big sky above, the distant harbor sounds, and the waves gently rocking me from side to side. I felt like I was in another country, a million miles from the city. And I discovered a community of families; some had lived there more than fifteen years. A real community.

I stayed for hours, read a book, fell asleep, and didn't leave till half past noon the next day. I loved the feel of it and I knew immediately this would be a perfect getaway from Manhattan *in* Manhattan, a hideaway for peace and quiet coming off the road from a gig. And I could paint and sculpt there with no distractions.

It was several days before I noticed that my new houseboat needed minor repairs that I had no clue how to do. I asked the dockmaster if there was anyone around who fixed boats.

He told me there was and that he would send him over the next time he saw him.

A day later, I was drawing in the quietness of the boat basin when I turned to see this huge burly man slowly zigzagging his way through a maze of gangplanks. I knew it must be him.

It was noon and I was sitting on the deck of the houseboat, getting ready to go to my office at MGM, when he walked right up to me and said, *"JIMI HENDRIX?"* He sounded like he was talking through a megaphone.

I looked at him and pushed down the urge to laugh. He was too big to laugh at. He looked mean enough to break me into little pieces.

"No, not Hendrix," I answered. *"Havens.* You know, R.H.; J.H. Havens. Hendrix. But . . . but . . . I can see where you might make the mistake," I said, knowing he didn't have a clue who I was—or who Hendrix was either.

"Yeah, well," he continued gruffly, "The guy up there told me some *rock guy* wanted his boat fixed."

"Yeah, he's right. I just got this thing and I want to know if it'll float or sink on me. I don't know if there is anything wrong with it. But if there is, I'd definitely want it fixed." I was leaning toward letting him start now if he could. "Could you look at it now?" I asked. "See if it needs anything major. I'm about to go to my office."

"Yeah, but if I see something right away, should I go ahead and *fix it?* And what if I spend money, man?"

"Just do your thing. I'll be back tomorrow at nine o'clock. If you spend anything, get a receipt and I'll take care of it."

So the next day I got back to the boat about ten-thirty and Michael, who looked like Hercules, was very unhappy, pacing all over the dock.

"You said you'd be here at nine . . . I got gigs to do, man . . . Where were you?"

"I'm sorry, but I was stuck at the bank and just couldn't get here. You know, slow subways, no cabs, New York traffic . . ."

"Okay, okay, that's okay, " he said and suddenly his deep booming voice lost its angry tone. "I fixed something," he said. "Cost me a hundred and fourteen dollars."

Without another word, I peeled off $114, gave it to him, and walked into the boat. He looked like he was in shock for a few seconds, but he did follow me on board.

"You don't want a *receipt*?" he asked.

"Is everything done?"

"Aah . . . no," he said.

"Well, when you're finished, you can give me all the receipts at once."

"There's some pictures there for you to look at. What you need to do on the boat," he said.

Pictures? I thought. *He has pictures of the work* and everything that needed repair? In less than twenty-four hours?

It turned out that Michael had more than a dozen 8x10s taken from every conceivable angle, showing this crack there and that electrical thing there, the broken alarm system, loose screws, you name it. Unbelievable. Every little detail needing to be patched or completely redone—even a crack in one of the engine blocks.

8x10s!

Crisp and sharp!

Getting 8x10s of anything in twenty-four hours was not easy, not unless you had your own professional darkroom.

Who is *this guy?* I asked myself. *You don't see the likes of him every day!*

Anybody who has a dozen 8x10s of a job he wants to do ready for review at nine o'clock the next morning is a trip. And that is exactly what Michael Sandlofer turned out to be. A trip across the ocean. A trip into things I never gave a thought about before he walked straight at me on that dock.

For the next couple of weeks, Michael and his two assistants were buzzing around my houseboat, fixing things from stem to stern. One called Little John made some jockeys I know look like Wilt Chamberlain. The other, Big Joe, was so huge he made Michael look like he was undernourished.

The real Bluto, I thought. *This guy* is *Hercules! And with a voice even deeper than Michael's.*

Little John was a useful guy to have on a boat. Nobody else could have gone straight down through the narrow trap door under the floor to untangle some wires and hoses. I couldn't believe any human being could fit in such a small space, much less work in it.

What a trio! And Big Joe was a little crazy.

One day he put on full scuba gear to go under the boat and take a closer look at the bottom. Unfortunately, it was low tide and I didn't realize that. Big Joe was so embarrassed he stayed underwater as if he was swimming under the boat, sending air bubbles to the surface for fifteen minutes, moving about on the bottom. If he stood up, the water probably wouldn't have been above his waist. Michael revealed that to me at least two months after we got to know each other. We laughed like hell.

Michael just happened to be fresh out of the Navy, a Vietnam vet who was one of the most respected hard-hat survey divers in the country, an author of many deep sea diving safety rules for OSHA when he was still in his twenties.

We got to know each other a lot better when he took me down to another houseboat nearby that he maintained weekly. It was a boat owned by a friend of his who had turned it into a small photo gallery that exhibited photos taken by inmates in maximum security prisons.

Michael didn't like many adults. He went into the Navy with phony papers at the age of fourteen and saw more than most men should see. The only way he kept his sanity was to keep his youthful innocence and do what he had to do, to survive the horrors. I probably was the last person he might have expected to trust. I looked like a hippie to him. But trust did come and later he told me it started from the moment I paid him the first $114 without asking him for a receipt.

"The only people I really trust are kids," he told me. "They don't have any malice against anybody." Michael worked in salvage, surveying underwater for private and official clients. All over the world.

Half-kiddingly, I asked him, "If you could have what you want, what would it be?"

"I'd like to have a museum for kids of my own that would teach them what is happening in the oceans and what we have to do to preserve it," he said.

I already knew enough about Michael to know that he responded sharply to challenges. Michael was action, not talk. Knowing this, there was nothing in this world that would keep him from getting what he wanted if someone could get his juices flowing.

"You really want a museum, Michael? If that's what you really want, all you have to do is ask for it," I said.

"What are you *talking* about?"

"Repeat after me. I want a museum. I want a museum. I want a museum."

"Here goes that hippie stuff," Michael said.

But I challenged him again. "No, what's the matter? Are you afraid? What I'm saying is that if you ask for it like I'm telling you, you better be ready for it, because it will come."

"Okay, okay, if it'll make you happy . . . *I want a museum, I want a museum, I want a museum.*"

No sooner did Michael speak those words than some real magic started to happen, the kind of magic that proves to me there is something going on out there—something cosmic and very real. Barely two days later he called me:

"How did you *know*?"

"What do you mean?"

"I got a house, a house in Nyack. How did you *know*?"

"I didn't know. You knew. You asked for it."

"A friend of mine called and asked me how would I like to have this house? I could do whatever I wanted to do with it. You're a *spooky dude,* Richie. I don't know about you," and he really meant that. It bothered him that something out of his control, or so he thought, could happen like that.

So Michael went ahead and opened his new house with the collection of sea artifacts he had collected through the years: sea turtle shells from South America, lanterns and ropes and shark jaws from all over the world, a lot of stuff. And while he was getting it set up I learned that Michael Sandlofer was a genius of a special kind.

"This teacher I know," he said to me one day, "she keeps bugging me to ask you if you would come over to her class and sing for her kids . . . She saw you on *Sesame Street* or something and she says you're pretty good . . . I don't know, maybe you are, maybe you can come over with me next week when I'm bringing something from the museum. You do sing for kids, don't you? How 'bout it? She keeps bugging me. Can you get this woman off my back? Okay?"

Of course I said yes. "What did you do for the kids in school?"

"I made a little museum for them in a classroom, like a natural history museum." Michael called them up and told them I was coming with him to sing a few songs.

It was more than a little museum. It was a major display of stuffed animals and bones, snakes, turtles of several kinds.

It took up space all around the room. It took an hour to go through if you stopped to read all the identification cards.

The back wall was the major attraction. It was a wall of tanks, floor to ceiling, like you see at most seaquariums. But the tanks were each inset into a panel box with a placard beaneath. AMAZON RIVER . . . and the tank contained plants, fish, stones, and so on, from the Amazon River. AFRICAN LAKE . . . and it was what you would find in an African lake. PACIFIC OCEAN . . . BRACKISH WATERS, and so on, and so on.

Not only did Michael construct a series of water tanks that brought these places to the kids, but, where the ATLANTIC OCEAN tank was set up, he made the water in it look murky, with miniature garbage cans and car tires and debris to illustrate the pollution endangering sea life today.

Michael certainly made brilliant aquatic environments, but his greatest gift was in knowing how to stimulate young, fresh minds to learn . . . below the surface . . . in every sense of the word. There was another thing going on in that school that Michael did not prepare me for and it led to a completely new way of looking at a certain group of people that rarely gets a fair shake. The class I was to sing for was a special class.

The class was for children with various handicaps and disabilities. It was, in fact, a class put together by a teacher who convinced the Brooklyn public school system *not* to exclude such kids from the regular public school curriculum. Michael, however, had not prepared me at all.

"Richie, don't worry if these kids don't seem to be paying any attention to you while you sing," one teacher said to me as I entered the room. There were twenty more teachers stand-ing against the wall. The whole staff knew I was coming, I guess. Some knew me from colleges I had played at before they became teachers.

"Most of these kids have a very short attention span— maybe a minute to a minute and a half," another teacher said. I felt a bit awkward hearing this. I could see the staff was there for a show, but I was picking up an attitude that also seemed to say: These kids probably will enjoy being entertained, but don't expect any of them to really listen to you.

Very quickly, though, I could see that these kids were a lot more in tune with their environment than the professional teachers standing up against the wall could recognize. While tuning my guitar, I started talking about how I learned a song, just like I do in my normal stage gigs. When I got to the place where most people laugh, every kid in the room laughed right on cue. Blew my mind.

"Maybe you know this song," I said. "It's called 'Kum Ba Yah'." I started.

"Kum ba yah, my lord, Kum ba yah.
Ohh Lor-d, Kum ba yah."

After a few lines, at least half the kids were singing right along with me.

They knew the words.

They knew the melody.

They sang right along with me. And a child in the back of

the room walked straight up to me, smiled at me, stood right behind me as I sang from a stool, and leaned up against my body with her arms around my waist. There was no disconnection. There was complete, total involvement, the closest and most natural form of communication in the world.

The teachers along the wall had their mouths open in stunned disbelief. And when we got through "Kum Ba Yah," I said, "Oh, I know another song. 'Row Your Boat'!"

They sang that one along with me too . . . For twenty solid minutes. Everybody in the room, including the teachers, was bawling between every verse. Me too . . . At the same time, some anger began to enter my thoughts.

A one-minute attention span? No way, man, no way!

Michael was looking at me strangely, as if I had somehow performed voodoo on these kids.

"What did you *do*?" Michael asked after the last song as a few teachers gathered around. "Michael, it wasn't me at all. I didn't do a thing. It's the kids themselves. All I did is what we all should be doing. We need to pay more attention to them," I said, looking directly at the two teachers who had spoken to me earlier. I was upset. Something had to be said.

"It isn't *their* attention span that's short. All of us need to look at *our* attention span for *them*. We all need to listen better to what they want us to hear."

When I finished explaining how I felt about all of this to Michael, he looked back at the kids in the classroom and thought about the way they looked at his undersea exhibits. He knew what I said was true.

So many people through the years tell us that people with disabilities can't learn or communicate with the rest of us.

YES, THEY CERTAINLY CAN. Maybe not as fast in some areas, but given the opportunities, given a little more effort from our side of the situation, *all* is possible. Literally so. So much has to do with the will to live. I should know. Two of my brothers are handicapped.

My brother Alfred hurt himself playing ball and he's paralyzed from the waist down. And my youngest brother, Leonard, lost his legs in a New York subway train accident during the winter of '97 . . . They found him in the tunnel. He was dragged down the tracks. But he's one of the people who continue to show me what the human spirit is all about.

I was in California when it happened. When I got to the hospital, I didn't think there was much chance he would make it. He was bloated and very, very weak. He looked horrible. I was in tears watching him lie there, thinking that his life was over. But just as I was leaving his bedside, he gently squeezed my hand to let me know he was still there. It was such a light touch that I wasn't even sure if I had imagined it. They said he was stable and needed to rest.

Three days later, I was back again from the West Coast and went up to see him, not sure there would be much difference.

I couldn't believe my eyes. Instead of lying there in a heap, Lenny was sitting up in bed, talking to two of his coworkers. Recognizable too. Gone was the bloated, puffy look. Leonard, the young man I knew, was there.

"A miracle," everyone said. If it was, it began the moment

God knocked him unconscious when the accident occurred. That left him without experiencing any pain while he was being mangled under the subway cars.

When he came out of his coma the next day, the damage already had been done. All he could remember was trying to go between cars on the train and having a seizure.

Sitting up in bed, he told me he would not let this thing stop him from living a full life. And he hasn't. Within a few weeks, he was all over the hospital in his wheelchair, and within a few months, they were making artificial limbs for him. It was his spirit that rallied him to keep going.

He was set on returning to work, getting around quite well, considering that he had looked so bad I thought he wouldn't make it. People can do anything they put their mind to. We all should know that by now.

It may not be easy for us to understand people who have all kinds of so-called handicaps, including those who seem incapable of what we think of as simple speech. But it is on us to learn how to tune into their languages, rather than the reverse. It isn't enough to rely on specially funded programs that isolate handicapped kids and miss the point completely. We need to open our minds and not be so quick to shut off opportunities for the so-called handicapped to socialize with the rest of us, without fear.

what does *extinct* mean, daddy?

Michael's passion for a maritime museum for kids was linked to an equal passion for whales as an endangered species.

"There's a whole lot you can learn about whaling in the whaling towns up and down the North American coast, but you'll have a hard time finding anything about the whales they caught," he said. He was right.

We went to a dozen towns on the coastline of Massachusetts and Maine and there were plenty of harpoons and fishing rigs and stories about the hardy men who caught these huge sea creatures for a living for hundreds of years. But there was nothing about the whales.

"Nobody really knows how the whale really lives, or communicates, or why some turn up on beaches half-dead, or what to do about that," Michael said. "There's a lot going on out there in the sea that affects all of us and it's going to be up to the next generation to take a hold."

I got caught up in Michael's idea, but most of all, I was turned on by giving kids the chance to learn about the world we live in, the world that we cannot afford to take for granted.

If our North Wind Undersea Institute, which was the name we gave to Michael's museum in Nyack, was going to become a meaningful place for kids to understand the sea, both of us would have to reach out to the community. That part wasn't hard at all.

Volunteers kept showing up at our doorstep, along with rare artifacts and manuscripts. It was almost as if we were supposed to make this museum work. Everytime we needed something, the next day we would get a phone call or someone would walk in with a trade for a missing piece of our puzzle. Rapidly we added to the booty Michael had collected in hundreds of dives through the years.

The museum was filling up with old tools and fading photographs, historic diving equipment and 100-year-old maps, shark jaws and whale bones, incredible scrimshaw and rare books, live crabs and turtles from several counties, and oceans, shells, books, and projects, little things to sell to keep the museum alive. Our first exhibit was going to be about whales. So we set out to find material for the displays.

After a somewhat disappointing trip to a Massachusetts fishing village, we could not believe our good fortune when Michael found himself sitting in a library at the same research table with a young graduate student who had just completed an extensive paper on whaling throughout American history.

He generously gave us copies of everything he had. Everything we needed.

From so little information about whales, we now had a library of information at our fingertips. Source material and photographs about different species, how they lived, what they did, where they migrated to, and which ones were endangered. But most of all, how whaling was historically tied to the making of America as a nation. It was the whaling captains who defended this nation. They were our first navy.

Michael also saw a retired tugboat in City Island junkyard and promised to remove it before the work week resumed on Monday. Yeah, right. Michael cut the boat in two, then hauled only the front end to the North Wind Undersea Institute and attached it to the museum's front entrance. This didn't make the junkyard owner very happy, but it gave us a perfect teaching tool, a full-scale "captain's bridge" with working communication equipment, harbor maps, navigation and steering gear. The kids loved it.

Dozens of schools throughout the tristate region now were booking the Institute for special tours and seminars. At the center of the Institute, however, was Michael's amazing talent to construct a wide assortment of underwater environments, each designed to display a different aspect of undersea life.

My brother Donald also got involved with beautiful drawings to complement the exhibits and I did some too. Michael even built a ten-foot "whale coffin," painted flat black, with rope handles on the sides and several reefs of flowers donated by local florists placed all around it. Plaques along the wall listed the name of each species under the picture, while pictures of extinct species were left blank. On purpose.

The exhibit was called "A Right to Live" and kids who walked into the museum with their parents invariably tugged at them when they noticed the blank pictures.

"Daddy, where's the whale that goes in the picture up there?"

"They're extinct."

"What does *extinct* mean, Daddy?"

"They ain't around anymore," the parent would answer. "They've died off."

And so would begin a deeper dialogue between parent and son or daughter.

The crucial points of the "Right to Live" exhibit were not lost on adults either. The director of the Explorer's Club—*the* Explorer's Club—saw it at the Nyack Library and immediately invited us to give a special presentation at a dinner for their membership in New York City.

The Explorer's Club is probably the most prestigious society of environmental scientists and adventurers in the world. Astronauts who walked on the moon were at that dinner, along with men who walked across Africa in the 1930s and some that had climbed the tallest mountains and most dangerous volcanoes on Earth. They were so moved by the humanitarian message and our attention to undersea detail that they asked to keep our exhibit on display for several weeks. They also extended us a rare honorary membership into the club.

Suddenly we no longer were just an ex-Navy guy and a

RICHIE HAVENS

At the North Wind Undersea Institute, devoted to homeless, stranded, and injured marine life. (*Photo by Steve Davidowitz*)

"hippie folksinger" with some wild idea to teach kids about the sea. Suddenly our North Wind Undersea Institute had the respect of the most important scientists and explorers in the world. Now our names and mission statement would forever be listed in the same logs with Charles Lindbergh, Admiral Byrd, Sir Edmund Hillary, and so many men and women who have advanced the cause of man's knowledge of this planet. Can you imagine the feeling?

"We've never seen the story of whales and their plight told any better than this exhibit," we were told. "The Explorer's Club applauds your efforts to educate young people about the sea and we are honored to pledge our support for your efforts."

In return, Michael and I knew we had to do even more to deserve this endorsement.

After taking "A Right to Live" to colleges in the Northeast and Midwest, we moved our North Wind Undersea Institute from Nyack in Rockland County to City Island on the Long Island Sound in the Bronx, where it remains to this day.* Like magic, dozens of people with special skills continued to knock on our door.

One of those special people was Laurie O'Gara, a friend of Michael's who was a pioneer woman member of the deep sea diver's union and also happened to be an expert metallurgist and welder—yes, a welder. She built several huge water tanks that allowed us to show how man works undersea in full gear. The tanks later were used to treat and work with a group of

*You can contact the Institute at 610 City Island Avenue, New York, NY 10464, 718-885-0701.

orphaned baby harbor seals we inherited from fishermen and conservationists in New Hampshire and Maine.

On January 13, 1982, we were watching on television the coverage of Air Florida Flight 90's crash into the icy Potomac River after a failed takeoff from Washington National Airport. It was a heartbreaking sight . . . Only four people survived that crash, even though many of the seventy-nine who died were alive on impact and drowned in the icy waters.

Michael said, "If there had been divers there, more people would have been saved. The only problem, divers can't be on call waiting for planes to crash. Especially in winter. *But seals can.* They should use seals for that kind of rescue."

Two years later, when the Institute inherited three baby seals, Michael recalled his idea and found an experienced dolphin trainer in California to come to work with him. They were able to train these seals to do three of the most amazing things I've ever seen. Now Michael had his search-and-rescue team—I believe the first to use seals in that way in the world. This, even after we were told by mammalogists that harbor seals could not be trained.

One seal could respond to fourteen different hand signals that sent him after fourteen different tools. Another learned to locate weapons and other objects on the ocean floor.

Still another was trained to dive below the surface to reach and unbuckle human beings trapped in their seats—from car and plane wrecks. This same seal was also trained to bring a small aqualung down to the victim, along with an apparatus we invented that allowed a balloon to be clamped on to carry the victim to the surface.

All three seals were trained to replenish their air from an underwater bell we invented so they could remain underwater with the victim or the working diver/trainer. Another world first.

It disturbs me to tell you, though, that despite several successful demonstrations of these revolutionary rescue techniques and some excellent publicity in *Life* magazine, *no organization, no airline, no branch of armed forces has found it worthwhile to seriously investigate using seals for their rescue potential*. In fact, the idea has been completely ignored to this day. Incredible.

That disappointment aside, we came to the conclusion that the best way to expose more kids to the Institute's undersea exhibits was to do it on the sea itself. So with some financial help from *Saturday Night Live*'s John Belushi and some other show business friends, Michael bought a rugged twenty-year-old fishing trawler in Holland and rigged it to teach about diving and to be an undersea museum with exhibits.

The Freedom Ship was our secondary museum space for more than a year while it was docked at the Fire Station Pier on Manhattan's East River. Unfortunately, a problem with the antiquated chain-steering mechanism left us with no way to take it up and down the East Coast as we had hoped.

Things were always happening around the Institute, however. One winter three whales were trapped under the polar ice in Alaskan waters and a group of our kids helped to save them.

RICHIE HAVENS

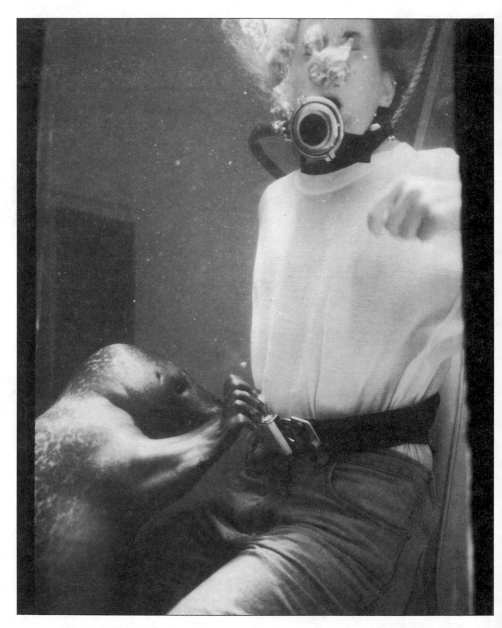

The *Life* magazine shot of a trained seal unbuckling an airline seat belt. Why they have not been deployed in real emergencies is something I will never understand. (*Photo © Frank Fournier/Contact Press Images*)

After talking about their plight, some of kids came up with an extraordinary suggestion: "The Coast Guard should drill holes in the ice and make sounds through the holes to help guide the whales to safe water."

We thought the idea was so good we sent the mayor of Barrow, Alaska, a set of instructional drawings that helped them free two of the whales, just as the kids described.

If you remember, Michael and I started the North Wind Undersea Institute around a strong belief that our best defense against environmental abuse is our youth. The North Wind Undersea Institute stood for very simple ideas:

- We are part of the same living system.
- To care about life in the sea is to care about ourselves.
- To endanger species in one part of the world is to impact life around the globe.
- We will strive to change the myths that continue to be taught to our youth.

To this day we continue to operate the North Wind Undersea Institute for kids of all ages. Yet I have to admit that I am disappointed in the way some of the obvious advances we developed have been ignored by those who need the help. The seals we trained for sea rescue is one such disappointment, and there is another that boggles the mind.

In the mid-1980s Michael and some of our most dedicated staff members developed an effective, very inexpensive method to get beached whales back to sea.

Now, everybody knows that whales are helpless when they beach themselves, but no one really knows why they do it. But I agree with Michael, who says it's "protest, pure and simple."

"They know they're dying and maybe they even know why they're dying . . . Maybe they come up to our shore to let us see for ourselves what we're doing to them. Maybe they are confronting us. Maybe the pollution is killing their young."

To get these huge helpless creatures back out to sea—either for a natural death or for a second chance at life—we successfully tested our own rescue method on beached whales in Baja Mexico with the cooperation of the Mexican government.

High-pressure hoses were used to force out a tunnel of sand underneath the distressed whale's head, tail, and midsection to place the harness and create narrow ditches to insert inflatable pontoons attached to heavy hemp. After the pontoons were filled, the whale was easily pulled back into the sea by three people.

It may be hard to believe, but after these successful tests and after Michael assisted in the rescue of a beached whale at Fire Island, nobody has bothered to use any of our techniques for whale rescue, even to remove whale carcasses. Sadly, this is an instance where practical ideas that could greatly advance the rescue of large sea mammals are being ignored by agencies that have struggled for solutions to the problem.

The reason? Nothing logical. In fact, the only reason we have ever been given is that The North Wind Undersea Institute is not part of any government agency, or university, or federally funded organization formally recognized to deal with such matters. How absurd is that!

Obviously, this is a sad commentary about a lot of things, but Michael and I remain encouraged by the many young people we have met through the years who do *not* share such blindness. That is why both of us believe so strongly that the damage done to the environment by the oils and machines of our age can be turned around by future generations.

This belief brought Michael and me together on that houseboat in Manhattan in the 1970s and it further led me to respond in 1990 to the community center and a minister of a church in New Haven, Connecticut, who wanted desperately to improve conditions in their neighborhood. With some prodding and support from me and later from multitalented, highly passionate Diane Edmonds, the kids themselves took amazing steps forward on behalf of us all.

The organization was called the Natural Guard, where kids challenged themselves to learn about every aspect of their environment, expressed their feelings in various art forms, prodded the community into cleaning up drug-infested neighborhoods, and grew food for their families and for the needy. They wrote and confronted senators and congressmen to enact important conservation laws and changed the direction they were headed.

President Bush had challenged youth organizations throughout the country to come up with a national program or project to increase awareness about the diminishing ozone layer. Five youth organizations, the Natural Guard among them, responded directly to the challenge by creating a "pledge sheet," a questionnaire on which people could check off things they could really do to help save the ozone layer. Items included "Ride your bike to the store, instead of driving"; "Turn off the lights you don't need to save electricity"; and so on.

For each item, the students calculated amounts of ozone that would be saved. So by checking off the things you pledged to do, you could add up how much each item contributed to your effort. Sign your pledge and off to President Bush it would go. At his request. But the kids went one step further. When they got 200,000 signed pledges, they brought it directly to the White House to add Bush's signature, as the president had asked them to do. Well . . .

President Bush rebuffed them, but the kids wouldn't leave. They wanted the president to live up to his half of the deal. Instead, Senator Al Gore (Tennessee), a Democrat, and Pete Domenici (New Mexico), a Republican, came to speak to the children in place of Bush.

The press heard about the attempted meeting with President Bush and showed up when Gore and Domenici met with the kids. The senators took the kids to the Senate floor, where they opened the first official youth meeting of the Senate in American history—with just the two of them there, of course.

The kids started the meeting this way: "We have nothing to say until you take the same oath we have taken to protect the environment."

The senators, thinking this was pretty cute, proceeded to

follow along with a young man's recitation of the children's environmental oath—line by line. The senators' faces changed drastically when they began to realize what they were committing to as the words came from their own mouths. They were committing—*publicly*—to preserving the environment.

At the end of the meeting, another young man summed up the way the kids saw President Bush's sense of priorities: "Yesterday the Redskins won a championship football game and I bet Mr. Bush will have plenty of time to see them."

He did.

The Natural Guard, like the North Wind Undersea Institute, started with a kernel of an idea to give young people a chance to learn about the world we live in and to contribute *now* and *later* to their own futures.

The Natural Guard may have begun with a dozen kids in one Connecticut neighborhood that needed a little encouragement, but it has expanded into a worldwide organization of effective young citizens who are an example to young and old alike. Indeed, two of the proudest moments of my life were to stand with many of these young men and women as they were awarded the presidential Points of Light Award and when young people stood by me when I was invited to read the Preamble to the United Nations Charter at the UN's fiftieth anniversary. It was broadcast to 114 countries.

I play music because it is my passion—my God-given way to communicate what I think and feel. But having helped start the Natural Guard and the North Wind Undersea Institute—having watched both organizations turn so many kids toward

RICHIE HAVENS

Addressing the United Nations with a group of children
from around the world.
(*UN/DPI photo by Evan Schneider. Copyright United Nations.*)

so many good things—I have learned that the most important thing any of us can do to improve this world is to *show it as it really is to our children*. The lessons from around the world are perfectly clear. We must regard our own communities as endangered environments. We need to involve our children on every level of rescue and conservation. They not only have the innocence to disregard the petty prejudices many of us have cultivated, but they are smarter than we were and more willing to make and be the difference.

getting a *"great blind degree"*

In the early 1970s I met Jack Hammer. He was a most unusual man with an incredible range of talents and he had just written a play about Jimi Hendrix. Jack was often mistaken for Jimi since he looked so much like him. Jack was deeply affected by Jimi's death, as were all of us who knew him. Jack's play was very impressive, a musical fantasy that had a lot of guts and really told Jimi's story through songs Jimi released as singles and through original music that Jack had written.

You may know Jack for the song "Great Balls of Fire," one of the most popular rock 'n' roll songs of all time. Jack wrote that song when he was sixteen and it became a smash hit for Jerry Lee Lewis only because Jack couldn't get it to Elvis Presley at Sun Records in Memphis, Tennessee. Otis Blackwell, who wrote several Presley hits, did get his hands on it and turned it over to Jerry Lee, who was also at Sun, to see what he could do with it. Not bad.

Jack was well named. A jack of all trades and master of a whole lot. Beyond songwriting, Jack was also a painter and one of the best tap dancers in the country. An actor too, an impersonator of rare skill, an imitator of many voices, and an improvisational stand-up comedian who could rattle off ten or twelve jokes about any name or word you could throw out at him.

Jack could do dozens of different characters and he sang and played guitar. He was a real trip, a real magician who got things done. That is, in fact, my definition of a *magician:* somebody who can take from nothing and get a song on the air, or a movie made, or play produced, or anything from the mind to reality. A magician. For real.

Anyway, Jack was about to accept a check for his Jimi Hendrix play for $15,000 from a well-known Broadway producer, when I convinced him that it deserved a whole lot more than that. We both thought it had great songs, strong dramatic elements, and a lot of movie potential. So we shopped around for financial backing to do it justice, but whenever we seemed on the verge of cutting a deal, there was always the stipulation that we would have to cast somebody "well known" or "change *this* or *that*" to bring in the money we needed. We decided not to sell out, not to do anything. To sit on it for a while.

About two years later—in 1974—Jack calls me up in Europe and says out of the blue, "Let's work on the play again and find a theater to put it on ourselves. Let's just do it."

The idea was good. So were the songs Jack had written for

the play, which was called *Electric God*. I was in, ready to produce it with my own money, when Jack called me up in Europe again to tell me he had found a theater—on Broadway, no less—for a weekend.

"A weekend on Broadway? How much?" I asked.

"Only four hundred dollars," Jack said.

"Four hundred dollars? That's impossible," I said.

"No, it's not," Jack answered. "We got it for Christmas Eve, Christmas Day, and the day after Christmas."

I groaned. "Oh, Jack, the place will be empty. Nobody's going to come to our show. New York is closed on Christmas."

"Let's do it anyway, Richie," he said. "We can record it while we're there. At least we'll have a good soundtrack for an album."

Not a bad idea at all.

So I came home and we put the play together. It looked and sounded great and we even hired David Infante, a young electronic whiz, to provide special effects from the balcony with his very inventive laser show—the first laser show on Broadway. Still, when Christmas Eve arrived, I was 100 percent certain we would be playing to ourselves. Most people were already at home with their families, having dinner, then getting ready to go to church. I thought, *No way anybody's going to come.*

Still, I was looking forward to finally seeing and hearing *Electric God* with all the production values in place. For one thing, Jack looked exactly like Jimi and there were wonderful things David did with his laser art. For instance, he projected a tiny blue butterfly that flapped its wings onto Jimi's guitar, the only light on the stage. Slowly, while Jimi (played by Jack) sang a blues tune, "If I Had Wings," the laser butterfly slowly grew larger and larger until the wings extended naturally from Jimi's shoulder. The scene was right before Jimi screws up and wrecks his hotel room before he's supposed to play Albert Hall in England.

So it was dark, about five-thirty in the evening on Christmas Eve, and I was running around all over the place, trying to make sure this and that were getting done for the few friends we expected to show up. I was upstairs in the balcony, looking at David's laser gear, when I saw the back window and impulsively looked out, straight up the block to Broadway . . . I was hypnotized by something I saw and by an idea that quickly came into my mind.

Looking straight up 45th Street to Broadway was the famous Camel cigarette sign with the amazing smoke rings coming out of the smoker's mouth, one every twenty seconds or so.

"David, do you have any mirrors?"

"Yeah, that's all I work with is mirrors," he said. "Why?"

"Just set one up here by this window," I answered. "And then let's aim one of those lasers at it."

David came over to see what I was looking at and together we adjusted the mirror so that the laser bounced right out the window straight up to Broadway right into the mouth of the Camel guy. And it started snowing!

What a sight in the night. A beam of light going right up 45th Street straight to the Camel sign directly through the smoke rings! All of a sudden people in the street began to look up at the sign and follow the strange beam of light right to the window of the 45th Street Theater.

Within an hour, enough tourists in the street followed the beam of light to our box office to fill the place. A sellout!

The crowd loved it and we sold out the next two days as well by word of mouth. The play got very good reviews from the few newspaper critics who saw it and we even got backing to produce it once more—for a special three-day showing at Town Hall the following year. While that too played to packed houses and good reviews, we never could get the backing we needed to put it on for a real Broadway run. Not unless we were willing to sell control of production and casting at the same time. As for the album, we still had the tapes. But the troubles I was beginning to endure with record companies going out of business all around me didn't help get the music out.

Oh well, no good work of art or good idea ever really dies and Jack eventually did put out an album for distribution on his Web site. Something tells me we still will get our chance to tell Jack's excellent Jimi Hendrix story. To this day, no one really has told Jimi's story correctly and Jack's play has the feel of a timeless piece.

The poster for Jack Hammer's fantastic Hendrix show, *Electric God*.

RICHIE HAVENS

Two Songs from *Electric God:*

WHO AM I

I've got myself a reason for living
don't need a reason to die
but with all this taking and giving
makes me wonder
who am I
what am I
and why am I.

I'm a man with a plan,
that's all I know
I'm a stone rolling on,
making friends
wherever I go.
I'm checking out the purpose for living
Somebody's just got to try
'cause all this pushing and shoving
makes me wonder
who am I
what am I
and why am I.

EARTH, MOON AND STARS

Take a shot of rain, snort some wind
turn off the pain, hello friend
love is in the sky, fire in the blood
man was born to fly,
don't drag him through the mud
Earth, moon and stars.

I can feel them beneath my feet
I'm gonna tell everyone I meet
take a love trip to Venus and Mars
Earth, moon and stars.

With two solid albums and a hit single out on the Stormy
Forest label, the same marketing employee who had alerted
me to the possibility of having my own label now was telling
me how I could protect myself from the common yet unethical
practice of underreported record sales.

"Sometimes they'll tell you they're going to send out fifteen thousand albums, but really they'll send twenty-five thousand and pocket the profits from the uncounted ten thousand
extra," he explained. "You're making these guys a lot of
money and most of the other labels are losing their shirts. You
should manufacture the albums elsewhere and sell them back
to MGM for distribution," he suggested. "That way you'll get
exactly what's coming to you."

Johanan Vigoda picked up the thread and got approval for

a provision that would allow us to take our master tapes to an outside company (Columbia) for pressing. Even further, MGM would be obligated to buy a minimum of 150,000 first-run copies. This meant that we would be paid for 150,000 albums (plus publishing fees, which are greater than royalties) as soon as they came off the presses.

This guaranteed a profit for Stormy Forest and put natural pressure on MGM to make sure our records got out to the stores. As most artists know, that's a big problem. Quite often, record companies just don't get the albums out on the shelves in time to do any good. Other times, they just sit on them for no good reason and the artist is put in a bind when he or she tries to negotiate a new deal. It's an old story and a sad one, but in this case, we had no worries, thanks to my "deep throat" inside MGM and Johanan, who got one other provision in the contract that no artist got before, not even the Beatles. The masters we made belonged to me, not MGM. This would prove to be very, very important a few years later when MGM was to find itself in serious financial trouble.

The third album and the first under the newly negotiated contract was *"The Great Blind Degree,"* with Eric (bass), Deano (guitar), Bob Margoleff (synthesizer), and Emile Latimer, an old friend from the Village, playing all the percussion instruments in place of Natoga, who went back home to Florida.

I got the title for *"The Great Blind Degree"* from a book I wrote on a long airplane ride, a book never published. It was a manual of unconsidered little things. Things our society has accepted or taken for granted without question, even though they never have been properly investigated or researched. For instance, Santa Claus.

The very minute Western civilization created Santa Claus it also created *no* Santa Claus.

By contrast and without intending any harm, those able to buy and give gifts *from* Santa Claus tend to put people who cannot afford the same gift-buying and gift-giving experiences in some discomfort, if not a disadvantageous light. While this may be seem trivial, that is exactly the point. It is an *unconsidered little thing* that exists and can be experienced differently, perhaps even hurtfully by some people while no one is paying attention. Those kinds of things separate us without our thinking about it. Class distinctions take root through such unconsidered little things.

"The Great Blind Degree" was about the extent to which we do not go to consider the consequences of the things we do, big and small. It was about how so many of us fail to prepare for letdowns and disappointments we could guard against in advance. The songs on the album reflected that and if I did not fully understand the point I was making in the book, the world I was living in was spelling it out for me every day.

I included "See Me, Feel Me" by the Who, "Teach Your Children" by Graham Nash, "Fire and Rain" by James Taylor, and "What About Me" by my old friend from the Village Dino Valenti. I understand through friends that "What About Me" became a personal favorite of San Francisco deejay, Tom Donohue, who played it often on KSAN during the Flower Power days.

"What Have We Done" also stood out on that album. It was written by Jeffrey Kauffman, a modern composer, and it was performed with full orchestra under Jeffrey's direction. But the song that really meant the most to me was "Think About the Children," written by Bobby Scott, who was from Brooklyn and who also wrote "A Taste of Honey."

THINK ABOUT THE CHILDREN

Why must we fight and put off deciding
who's right or who's wrong until tomorrow
Oh how much time can we borrow.
It's getting kind of late,
it's getting kind of late,
and don't you think it's time
we thought about the children,
thought about the children.

Why must we wait for some distant date
for things that are worse
Oh worse than dying
oh I hear somebody crying
it's getting kind of late,
it's getting kind of late,
and don't you think it's time
we thought about the children,
thought about the children.

Oh conceived and taught to say their prayers
and when we leave them,
we leave them with very little
in this world that's really theirs,
that's really theirs now
oh babies arrive just love them,
just love them and keep them alive
oh alive until tomorrow
for them tomorrow comes much faster
it's getting kind of late,
it's getting kind of late,
and don't you think it's time
we thought about the children,
thought about the children,
thought about the children,
Oh think about the children,
think about the children,
think about the children,
all over the world,
all over the world.

I took the band to Rio de Janeiro in Brazil to perform that song at an annual song and performance competition involving forty countries. The promoter who organized it originally tried to get Dylan to contribute a song, but when that didn't happen, Bobby Scott's "Think About the Children" was chosen. I was supposed to have it for a month before our trip, but actually only got to see it an hour before the jet took off. I learned it on the plane.

After our performance became the first American entry to win any award there after many years of American acts getting booed off the stage for political reasons, we were invited to the American Embassy for a celebration. We learned only then that they had been fearful for our safety.

In Europe and South America there are many such competitions. They last for days and are broadcast live over extensive government-supported television networks. There is no private commercial TV in some of these countries. Even so, the people themselves vote right in their living rooms and awards are given for best song, best singer, and best interpretation of a song. While I would not like to see government-controlled TV in America (commercially controlled TV is restricting enough), I would like to see such competitions on the networks. Real competitions, not merely popularity contests. I think we would see our greatest artists putting on the performances of their lives.

With the money from *"The Great Blind Degree"* and previous record sales, I bought my parents a new home in Brooklyn as well as lots of technical equipment that I needed to develop a number of other creative projects.

I really wanted to produce some television shows. I had a lot of extremely funny, multitalented friends who were natural improvisational actors. I taped them often enough to put together a good pilot for a show idea I was developing, but something kept getting in the way of completing a serious proposal.

As often happens in life, it was not too long after the idea was put on hold that Lorne Michaels put together the *Saturday Night Live* troupe and created a show that was nearly exactly what I had in mind.

Having already purchased three very expensive industrial videotape cameras at a time when the technology was so new that only the big television studios could afford them, I was always looking for ways to use them. Among other things, I did the first videotaping of karate lessons for public distribution. Ron Van Cleef and Ron Taganasi were black belt masters who helped me with this and both were pretty surprised to learn that I was mostly self-taught in karate, having practiced the basic stances and movements I saw in books. Karate was excellent self-defense, but even more powerful to harness one's own inner discipline.

The visual side of me has been a part of me since I was a child. I did not stop drawing when I picked up the guitar. Every so often I get an urge to draw or paint or, in recent years, use my computer or some combination of those tools to create something from my mind's eye.

In fact, one of the things I do from time to time is sketch with *my eyes closed* and with both hands at the same time. I do it to help me stay within myself and to release my energy in a direction it takes itself. This is not an exercise. Often, the attempt to sketch a face, using just my mind's eye and a few colored pencils with my eyes shut reveals a feeling behind the image.

After *"The Great Blind Degree,"* my next album was another

An example of my two-handed, eyes-closed sketch style.

double album, a compilation we put together of live performances recorded while I was touring. Called simply *Richie Havens on Stage*, it was the largest recorded sampling of my live performances I would ever put together, but it came at a time when the financial roof began to fall on MGM.

One day I walked into the MGM Building and saw a mechanical ad poster for the current MGM hit movie *Goodbye, Mr. Chips* sitting on the reception desk. Mr. Chips was seen scurrying gingerly across the poster, briefcase swinging in hand. A handwritten message was scrawled over him that made everything crystal clear.

GOODBYE, EVERYBODY the note said. The receptionist wasn't just wishing all the MGM employees her own private goodbye. The whole staff had been let go. MGM had closed down every subsidiary label in the building except for two. Casablanca Records had Spanky and Our Gang and Stormy Forest had me. All the lawyers were gone, all the secretaries were gone, all the studio technicians were gone too. Everybody was gone from the three floors of the MGM offices.

We were the only ones left. The company was slashing costs and preparing itself for an all-out sale. My next album, *Richie Havens Portfolio*, was going to be delayed almost a year by the turmoil and even though it did just as well as *"The Great Blind Degree,"* we went to the office every day knowing things were not going to last.

Three different presidents had passed through the executive suite in less than four years, including twenty-one-year-old whiz Mike Curb, who tried to put a charge into the scene but was just too inexperienced to make a difference. Curb had risen to such heights so early in life after making a series of successful commercials.

He started out on the wrong foot, by putting the banner on the already released *Mixed Bag* that boasted: FEATURING THE HIT SONG FROM WOODSTOCK: "HANDSOME JOHNNY." This may have seemed like a good marketing tool to him, but it upset me because it was like saying "new and improved," as if the album needed any phony hype.

After assuring me that he wanted to support Stormy Forest, Curb asked me to add music to a very avant-garde movie MGM was putting out. He said we could use our own Stormy Forest songs. We were going to get a big break here, we thought. The film was very intriguing—a hard-hitting, offbeat piece that was way ahead of its time. We were pretty excited about it. So was the director when he heard the music we put to his film. Each song seemed to fit perfectly with the scenes they were placed in.

On opening night in New York, however, we could not believe what the company execs had done to this film. They took all the edge from it and turned it into a royal mess. The end was moved to the middle, the characters were changed, and nothing in it made any sense at all.

The film was awful. So bad we sat in the theater in complete shock, unable to speak. Even the title was an absurd joke: *The Magic Garden of Stanley Sweetheart.*

The critics in the morning papers tore it apart: "the worst movie of the year"—and that was the best review it got. We knew we had to do something—fast. We didn't want our music used like that. The director was angry at what had happened to his movie, but he couldn't do anything about it. We could.

After Mike Curb looked at the situation, he set up a meeting with the head of MGM Pictures, who agreed that we had been wronged and promptly ordered every print to be recalled to remove our music as we requested. An honorable move, but a major disappointment to us, nonetheless.

Back on the twentieth floor, the once-active MGM offices were so deathly silent I could hear and *feel* the underground subway cars rumble 250 feet below me. Bernice got tired of bringing books to read to work and went back to Brooklyn. Even Mark was bored. Nothing was happening; nothing was going to happen until the new ownership took over.

That didn't occur until MGM realized it had to buy out my contract and give me the master tapes to clear the way for the sale. A German-based company, PolyGram, made the deal and that brought Jerry Schoenbaum into my life again. While I no longer had my own label, Jerry had been hired by Poly-Gram to run their new American presence, Polydor. Jerry promptly offered me a recording contract.

This lasted for one album, *Mixed Bag II*, which we laid out to parallel our first album together, *Mixed Bag*. The best song on it was "Indian Prayer," written by Roland Moussa, a very young songwriter at the time. Roland put it together from the various Indian treaties that had been broken. It had the eternal language used in the treaties and the reverence of a hymn. It was a consciousness-raising song.

RICHIE HAVENS

When I finished *Mixed Bag II*, late in 1974, I thought it was the best album I had ever done. Unfortunately, Jerry was unhappy with the decisions being made by the new German-based owners and quit. There was too much confusion and very little understanding of the American music business and the album was left hanging out there with little promotional support, so I left too. This would lead me to the strangest and most expensive recording adventures of my life.

from the twentieth floor to
common ground

J erry Moss and his partner Herb Alpert, the popular trumpet
player, owned an ambitious record company, A&M Records.
Just as Jerry Schoenbaum's Verve Folkways and Verve Forecast labels had provided me with a boost, Alpert and Moss
wanted to give new and undersupported artists a real chance
to develop a following. For seven years, Jerry had offered me
a place on his label. I had a meeting with him and we came
to an agreement.

We cut a deal for two albums. The first, *The End of the
Beginning*, was supported with a full concert tour, complete
with a band they paid for and all the promotional support it
deserved. Yet, upon hearing the song "I'm Not in Love," which
Jerry's wife loved, he thought we should release that as the
single.

I asked them specifically not to release that song as the
single, though. It already had been out there as a huge hit for

10cc and I thought it would not be played on the radio so soon after its first big run. I asked them to release "Daughter of the Night" instead, a beautiful song I got when someone just handed me a tape of it in Sweden. But A&M went ahead and released "I'm Not in Love" anyway. As I anticipated, it went nowhere.

Still, the album itself was very satisfying and did quite well. Among other things, the great rock 'n' roll band Booker T. and the MGs got back together for this record and backed me up on several cuts, including a Dylan love song, "If Not for You."

But in 1977, after getting approval for another lengthy tour to support my second album for A&M, I returned to find that the man who had approved the two-month European trip was gone from the company and no one was willing to stand up and pay the $87,000 travel tab I had personally charged to my credit cards. They just stuck me with the bill and I was left to pay it off myself during the next several years. I guess the title of this album was a bit prophetic: *Mirage.*

In 1980 I turned my attention again toward the video arts and the new technologies that were being developed on a daily basis all around me—in music, in television, and in motion pictures. I already had three early vintage videocameras and knew there was much more to be created artistically using the new tools, especially by the talented people I was meeting.

I formed a company with my business manager, Marcia Wolfson, who did a great job organizing my finances at a time when I badly needed that, and with a talented fine artist and graphics designer, Arnold Clapman. We believed that the artist was destined to be in the forefront of the computer animation field. We felt the new technology could be used most effectively by artists.

ARM (*Arnold*, *Richie*, and *Marcia*) was set up to do several things that had not been done before.

First, we developed plans for the first all-digital studio for sound *and* video *and* digital computer programs. The studio would be able to completely restore old films. In addition, the digital computer would feature eight layers of animation with eight levels of time control and eight separate light source controls. ARM would have the capacity to create entirely new media—all of it 100 percent real-time digital.

I had seen so many old films deteriorating and realized that the emerging computer technologies could be used to repair and restore scratches, fading, and contrast. ARM was to be the first all-digital studio . . . in the early eighties! Way ahead of the vision of those who thought they were on the cutting edge. What we proposed still does not exist.

ARM also perfected a colorization technique that was better than anything ever used, including those in vogue today. And we did a successful Rotoscope demonstration for Cheech Marin of Cheech and Chong, who bought the rights to an animated version of a book titled *The Ronin*, a Japanese story. We did about 15,000 separate cells for Cheech that lasted all of eight seconds on the screen—that's how precise it was. RKO even gave us a substantial portion of 35mm footage from the original *King Kong* and we completely repaired several kinds of damage to prove the value of our techniques. Several movie companies saw our work and wanted us to begin doing projects for them, but we were grossly underfinanced for that kind of operation.

The highly refined technical equipment we needed to execute sufficient contract work for major clients was close to $6 million, well beyond our private means at the time. And every time a different company inquired about a slightly different need for our process, we had to fine-tune our proposals and demos at greater personal expense. So, lacking a wise benefactor or a company or major bank to underwrite our full-scale start-up costs for this new technology, we were left with our inventions and no place to run with them. That is still where we are with this restoration technology. Capable, but not funded. The experience also paralleled some of what I was enduring in my roller-coaster recording career.

Through most of the 1980s into the mid-1990s, I recorded several albums for a handful of companies and repeatedly found myself up against changes in management, weak distribution, and other problems of the business.

Connections was to be the first of a two-album deal with Elektra-Asylum. But as Yogi Berra is famous for saying, it was "déjà vu all over again." Just as MGM had done, Elektra fired most of its employees when the first record was due to come out, including the president. The new people distributed a few token copies to a handful of cities and buried it on the shelf. They didn't care what was on the record. They didn't want anything developed by the people they had replaced to do well.

THEY CAN'T HIDE US ANYMORE

When something like that happens, there is no recourse—unless you own the label or the masters, which I no longer did. I owned the publishing rights to the songs I wrote, but not the recordings that lay on those shelves, gathering dust.

It took me three years to even think about getting involved in another record deal. When I did, I did it myself. In Europe, where my albums always sold well. They still do.

Common Ground (1983) was a wonderful project, a collaboration with Pino Daniele, a truly great Italian singer-songwriter and master guitarist who revolutionized popular music in his country. He was the angry voice of the Italian youth. He wrote songs that challenged the status quo and the traditional forms of long Italian musical progressions. Pino used American phrasing in his songs, with the pure Neapolitan dialect.

We met because I heard him sing on the radio and I asked my Italian road manager to arrange a meeting. She said, "He's recording right now in Milan and that's where we're going to be on the last stop of your tour. I'll see if I can arrange it."

We met and hit it off right away, and agreed that we would try to work together the next time I came to Italy. A year and a half later, the time was right.

Pino invited me to spend ten days working with him in his own private studio near his home in Formia to develop a few songs for a collaboration. In a nearby hotel, I wrote and worked on the first song. He had written a chorus, which I wrote verses to. I brought it down to his house the next morning to show it to him. We found out right away that there was magic going on between us.

Pino spoke very little English, but when he saw what I had written, he was spooked. He brought out the notebook with the chorus he had give me and on the same page he had written some attempts at the first verse.

We had written the same first line!

We wrote five songs in those first ten days and agreed further to get together again to do an album. *Common Ground*. This was the song we wrote together that had the same first line.

MOONLIGHT RAIN

Got up this mornin'
and I started on my way
I set out to find you
been searching for days and days
And when the sun would finally go
and the night would surely come

It's a Moonlight . . . it's a Moonlight
it's a Moonlight Rain
it's a Moonlight Rain coming down.

I can tell anybody
if they really don't want to know
all I really could hope for
is that all my loving shows
But I find myself walking all alone
and I am hoping the pain would go

but it's a Moonlight . . . it's a Moonlight
it's a Moonlight Rain
it's a Moonlight Rain coming down . . . on me

How I wish I could tell you
about the love that I feel inside
It's my love I would give you
it's my love that I cannot hide
Yet I hear a voice keep saying
aren't you sorry that you lied

Cause it's a Moonlight . . . it's a Moonlight
It's a Moonlight Rain
i'ts a Moonlight Rain coming down on me.

The recording studio where we did this album actually was
a remodeled Borgia castle from the Middle Ages, an ideal place
to get my head together, write songs, and gather my thoughts.
We recorded it for EMI Italy, where it was a major hit.

Five months into my stay, while we were in the final stages
of the album—in-between Pino's European tours—I learned
what it felt like to be recognized by *everybody* everywhere. It
happened in the town of Bari, where the annual Battle of the
Record Labels took place for five days. Bari was an industrial
town, a workers' town, not a resort, but it did have a memorable theater, one of the oldest in Europe, an absolutely incredible oval theater, with box seats from floor to ceiling, maybe
eight stories tall.

RICHIE HAVENS

The Battle of the Record Labels was a team competition similar to the individual competitions in Brazil. In this case, a nationwide television audience would vote for the team of their choice and awards would go to the label that had won. Each label was allowed one "foreign representative," and EMI sent me. It was the biggest television show of the year in Italy. It lasted five days and was seen by everybody in the country. And I do mean everybody. The audience was huge.

I was waiting offstage to appear, holding a wireless microphone in my hand upside down, waiting my turn. One of the sound technicians for the broadcast was worried. He came over and gently tried to get me to turn the microphone over. I acknowledged him with a smile, saying, "I know, I know, it's upside down."

He didn't speak English.

A few times during the next fifteen minutes he returned and we went through the same silent conversation. Finally it was my turn to go on and as I was walking onstage, I suddenly realized I was in trouble.

All music on Italian TV at the time was lip-synched. There was no live music at all and the song I was going to sing had no musical intro to give me a chance to get in synch. Without thinking, I raised my hand with the microphone to my mouth and realized, of course, that I was still holding it upside down.

Lucky me.

The upside-down microphone was blocking the camera's view of my mouth. When the music began, I flicked my wrist and pulled the correct end toward me. It was an accidental dramatic movement that caught everybody's attention and it gave me the split second to get into synch with the music that had started half a beat before I was ready.

The next day people recognized me everywhere I went. And I mean everywhere. Dozens of people gestured to me—in shops, from across the street, looking out the windows of buses, in hotel lobbies—as if they were holding a microphone upside down. And they continued the pantomime by flipping the imaginary microphone upright with their wrists. They all were amused by this unusual way to hold a mike and they were somehow impressed by it. It became my signature in Italy. To this day when I sing anywhere without a guitar, I will usually hold the microphone in this unorthodox way. Actually, the more I did it, the more it felt perfectly natural. It is a great way to hold a mike perfectly steady.

Back in America, I distributed *Common Ground* on my own with some friends who were independent promotion people. We took it ourselves to record shops in several major cities where it sold thousands of copies with a limited promotional budget. It's still one of my favorite recordings and Pino Daniele remains one of the most respected artists in Europe.

In 1986 I cut a deal with Rykodisc to do two CDs. One was a compilation of songs from my Stormy Forest catalogue, the other was to be a complete set of my favorite Beatles and Dylan tunes, a project I had wanted to do for years. It was going well in the studio, when the agent who made the deal sent the preliminary tapes to an executive at Rykodisc who made the unbelievable mistake of releasing them—*as is*. None of the tracks had

The first time I held the microphone this way, it was a mistake. But it felt natural, and now I do it all the time. *(Photo by Leslie Hawes)*

full instrumentation, not even a live drum! He sent tapes that had a drum machine playing on it. The piano player and I had used the machine only to lay down the tracks. We had intended to replace it with a real drummer in our next sessions.

This was a completely innocent mistake, but a dumb one, made by someone who had no idea what he was listening to, and it left me with no chance to complete the project in the right way . . . Strangely, some people still come up to me in concert and tell me how much they enjoy that album—even though it was barely half-done.

In 1987 I met some owners of a successful classical label who wanted to venture into the pop market. They said they were only going to sign one or two performers and go slow, but after they signed me they went wild and signed quite a few more and were quickly overextended in every direction. They went under in a year. While the album I had done for them—*Simple Things*—was out in the marketplace doing well, suddenly they went under and there was nobody there to pick up the slack and go on. My new publishing and production company, ELO Productions, was in no position to suddenly become a major record label.

It wasn't too long after *Simple Things* that I got a call from Johanan, who told me that he had a shot at starting his own label. I was happy for him; he loved great songs. Then he told me that he wanted me to be the first performer on it.

Dick Griffey, a friend of Johanan's, was going to help him put it all together. I knew Johanan for almost thirty years and trusted him, so I signed a deal with him. It turned out, however, that Dick Griffey didn't do much to get Johanan started but did convince him to record me on Griffey's Solar label as a prelude to something between them down the road. Solar was distributed by Sony, which sounded good, but Dick never mentioned that he was at war with Sony at the time.

The album was called *Now* in its original form and was going nowhere while Solar was fighting Sony. In fact, while Johanan was desperately negotiating separate deals to distribute *Now* in various European countries, I saw the album released in America under a different title, *Yes,* with a tune by that name added to the original song list. All this was done without my permission, of course, and no royalties have ever been paid to me since its release.

Around this time I immersed myself once more in my visual arts, which have been enhanced through the logarithmic explosion of computer and video technology.

On Location Systems was based on an idea I had been carrying with me since I saw my first 360-degree movie screen in the early 1960s, I believe at the Kodak Pavilion on the site of the World's Fair in New York City. My idea was not going to require millions of dollars of equipment or miles and miles of film to make forty-minute films for museums and world's fairs. Along with my partner in OLS, Richard Savage, a man with a brilliant scientific mind, I thought we could provide a unique variation of the 360-degree movie screen by arranging eight video cameras in one central location—facing outward—to shoot a full panorama. This technology offered many applications. The most important to me was education and rehabilitation. It offered unlimited commercial applications as well.

We envisioned using OLS as a possible setting for a restaurant, or even a movie theater, in which the diners or movie audience would get the same panoramic view they would get if they had been in the spot where the cameras were set up.

Imagine sitting in a basement restaurant where you could be seeing the exact view one would see from the top of the Empire State Building. Or the Eiffel Tower. In every direction, complete with normal, natural movements. We designed a modular vehicle that we registered as the Place Station—the

OLS Place Station—which we used as our basic presentation system.

Maybe an architectural company would want to set up a conference room with actual panoramic views of specific construction sites. Or perhaps your family doctor would hope to improve the ambience of his reception area with the scenic wonders of the world. Our enclosed 360-degree environment with eight large TV monitors was going to be able to do that.

I even wrote a screenplay for the idea. A screenplay called *Hostage* that involved a hijacked aircraft, in which the perspective of the audience would be from a seat aboard the airplane and would be as captive as the actors in the film.

If gunshots were to be fired in that setting, you could bet that the audience would duck. And speaking of betting, sometime later the New York Racing Association saw the merit of having one of our OLS Place Stations as an indoor viewing room where the race would take place around you as if you were in the infield. But I guess we missed the photo finish. The idea was put on hold while the NYRA's annual political battles flared up with the state over their operating budget. So went another brainstorm that I'm still working on. Among other things, I am convinced it will be the classroom of the future.

Things began to change—finally—when I signed a deal in 1994 with Rhino Records to put out a compilation called, appropriately, *Résumé: The Best of Richie Havens*. Rhino, a specialist in the field of compilations, did an excellent job with this collection.

While I have enjoyed playing to packed houses all over the world for many years, my recording career certainly has been a roller-coaster ride. Yet whenever my albums have been out there in the stores, they have sold quite well even without substantial promotional support. *Résumé* sold well enough to encourage Rhino and me to do a new album in the studio, the first time they ever put out an album of new recordings. The album, *Cuts to the Chase,* was released in 1995 and would become my bestselling album in many years. I produced the album myself in Phoenix, Arizona, in a private home studio.

Among other highlights was Jackson Browne's "Lives in the Balance," and the band behind me was loaded with talent. Chuck Mangione played flugelhorn, Jimmy Mack was on bass, Ed Barretini played drums, Louis Small and Paul Chansky were on keyboards—Paul's brother Greg Chansky played guitar on the two songs he wrote—and Billy Perry, an incredible blues guitarist, completed the band. In 1998 Billy would join me on the Bethel stage for the A Day in the Garden festival and blow the crowd away with his amazing rendition of Jimi Hendrix's historic version of "The Star-Spangled Banner."

In fact, both *Résumé* and *Cuts to the Chase* continue to sell at a steady pace. So does *Mixed Bag,* as do the rest of my recordings still in circulation.

miracles in the middle east

On November 21, 1977, Jack Hammer and I were watching an historic event on TV in my New York office: one of the most significant things to happen in the twentieth century. President Anwar al-Sadat of Egypt landed in Israel. We knew it was a daring thing for him to do. No Arab leader had ever attempted such a bold step. But little did we know that we would soon be caught up in the event ourselves.

What impressed both of us right away were the tears of joy on so many Israeli faces—young and old. They didn't hide their emotions at all. They understood the courage of this Egyptian President who was bringing them a daring peace initiative. Here was a Middle East leader coming with peace after his own government had sworn to destroy Israel since it was created in 1948.

"It doesn't look to me like these people want to do any

RICHIE HAVENS

A sketch I did of Anwar Sadat, the great champion of peace.

harm to that man," I said to Jack. "Just look at them. It doesn't look like any of them want to make war."

"The papers make you think he's heading into the lion's den. But look at the smiles on their faces," I said. "*People* don't make war, governments do. Who knows? Maybe this act of courage by this leader, this human being, really will give peace a chance."

Both Jack and I talked on and on about the importance of this event to our own American interests—how attached we all are to the fate of the Middle East. World history. Religion. Oil. None of us can escape the fact that we're forever linked to what goes on there.

After that peek into world history as it was being made, I felt a strong urge to write a song about the situation—a song that might help Americans understand what was happening. Apparently, Jack was feeling the same thing, because the second I mentioned it, he went off to a desk and sketched out some lyrics. That's what songwriters do.

Jack's instant lyrics were amazing as usual and I worked out the chord progressions just as quickly. The whole thing almost wrote itself and after we went through it a few times, I turned to him and said, "We've just got to put this thing down *right now*, Jack. *Tonight*. It feels like a really good song."

So I called a friend, Malcolm Cecil, a wonderful jazz bassist I knew who also engineered a recording studio in Manhattan right next door to Studio 54, the famous disco club, and he quickly invited us over to work after a recording session that was still in progress.

When we got there, I was stunned to silence when I poked my head inside the studio and saw the band in session. Not only was it a group I had played a few gigs with some years earlier in Europe, but considering the song we came to record, it was mind-blowing to really see them sitting there—a *Syrian*, a *Persian*, a *Saudi*, and an *Israeli*—playing together. They went by the name Les Variations and while they had previously had enormous success in Europe as a rock band, here they were recording new music with *Middle Eastern instruments!*

Now, that's pure magic, I thought. *Who else to record this song with!*

A few hours earlier, Jack and I were just sitting around watching the tube and here I was, recording a "peace song" about the Middle East with this virtual *United Nations* band playing Middle Eastern instruments. How perfect was that! And it wasn't even half the story.

The song was recorded in one straight take, mostly because the rabbi in the band barely had twenty minutes before sundown Friday would begin his strict observance of the Jewish Sabbath. No other take was needed. We hit it all the way through as if we had been playing it all our lives. It was called "Shalom, Salaam Aleichem," which is simply the universal greeting of "Hello, goodwill to you, and farewell" in Hebrew *and* Arabic. *Shalom* is the Hebrew form of the greeting and *salaam aleichem* means the same thing in Arabic.

Knowing that my friend Malcolm still had plenty of mixing to do for Les Variations, I went behind the glass and told him not to worry about dubbing me a copy until tomorrow or the day after. Jack and I left feeling as if we had done something really special.

The next day I was sitting in my New York office when Marcia Wolfson, my business manager, picked up the phone and I could hear her say, "The Egyptian Embassy? You want to talk to Richie? Is this some kind of joke? Just a minute."

So I picked up the phone and listened to an Egyptian consul say he had just listened to the song I recorded and would I come to Egypt and sing it?

"When?" I asked.

"We would like to make arrangements for you as soon as possible. Will you go? Yes?"

The words were barely out of the consul's mouth when my other phone rang and I could hear Marcia say, "The Israeli Embassy? You want to talk to Richie? You're not kidding, are you? Just a minute."

So here I was with a phone in my right ear, saying yes to an invitation to go to Egypt to sing "Shalom, Salaam Aleichem," and with another phone in my left ear, accepting an invitation to sing the same song in Israel! How surreal.

Malcolm, God bless him, was behind all of this. After he dubbed our tape past midnight, he had sent copies to the Israeli and Egyptian embassies.

Travel to the Middle East was complicated. There are laws about crossing into Arab countries directly after stopping in Israel. And there were equally sensitive travel issues in Israel. So I was not actually able to go to Egypt to sing this song, but it helped that the man who invited me was Prime Minister Mamdouh Salem, head of the peace-negotiating team under Sadat, and formal negotiations were about to begin.

The Israeli government arranged for me to be interviewed and to sing the song *live* on Israeli television one day and as a concession to the minister's standing with the peace talks, the Israeli government gave him unprecedented approval to bring an Egyptian television crew to Israel to interview me and let me sing the song for Egyptian TV.

RICHIE HAVENS

SHALOM, SALAAM ALEICHEM

The dove of peace
has flown to Israel
to calm the troubled waters
and ring the freedom bell.

No more must war
destroy this Holy Land.
Let the rain fall on the desert
and love bloom in the sand.

Shalom, Salaam Aleichem,
Shalom, Salaam Aleichem,
Shalom, Salaam Aleichem,
Peace be with you forever.

"Shalom, Salaam Aleichem" was released as a special re-cording with 100 percent of the proceeds donated to the Peace Now students' organization at Jerusalem University. It was a number-one hit in Israel for years, where it continues to be played on the radio almost thirty years later. But that too is less than half the story. The rest came after my initial Israeli TV appearance. In Jerusalem.

When I first got off the plane, I remember thinking, *Well, Grandma, we made it.* My grandmother always wanted to make the journey to the Holy Land.

I did an interview with General Moshe Dayan's daughter,

who was a news correspondent, and there were a couple of sold-out university concerts and some television shows hastily arranged by an Israeli promoter. But that was only my ticket to really see Israel up close, to meet some very extraordinary people.

I jammed with a number of great Israeli jazz musicians who seemed to show up in my hotel room practically on cue. I went to the Wailing Wall and to Christian and Moslem shrines, and I sat for hours in cafes, studying my books and the tomes on astrology and the religions of the world that I carried with me for years.

Here I was in the region that spawned Judaism, Christianity, *and* the Moslem faiths, watching a modern society blend with the ancient traditions. I was in no hurry to go home.

I ran into Abbie Nathan, an amazing Israeli whom I had known briefly in New York. Abbie was the guy who bought a pirate radio ship and went to the South Pacific to pump peace songs to both sides of the Vietnam War. After a couple of bankruptcies—pacifism can be expensive, you know—Abbie was back with a new ship, broadcasting peace songs to the Arabs and Israelis a few miles out in the Mediterranean. He had, in fact, the only offshore radio station in the eastern Mediterranean. Back in the States, I had performed on his boat in New York Harbor to raise funds for his first mission to Vietnam.

Abbie also had his own private plane now, a Piper Cub, and he was using it to fly to Egypt to bring his peace message direct to the people there. The border patrol tried to discourage him for months, but gave up. Whenever Abbie flew into some desert landing strip in the meeting zones, they just shook their heads as if to say, "Here comes Abbie again." A lot of Egyptians welcomed Abbie's peace missions. But most wished he would just stay home, rather than listen to him or his music.

You had to admire Abbie. He spent his whole adult life as a passionate believer in the goodwill of men—a freelance peace missionary who spent all his own money to go to the world's hot spots simply to talk with people and share songs of peace from all over the world. Many people probably looked at him like he was the man in the Martian movies who approaches the space invaders and says, "There is nothing to fear from us. We come in peace." But if you ask me, being a freelance peace missionary took a lot of guts. Quite a thing to be in the latter half of the twentieth century, I think.

Abbie asked if it would be okay if he interviewed me for his *Peace Ship* radio show. I agreed, of course, so the promoter took me the next day to a small recording studio in Tel Aviv, where we recorded the interviews.

With the promoter standing ten feet away, Abbie taped a good interview about the world we live in and the song Jack and I wrote, but then he cracked a wry smile and put the promoter squarely on the spot.

"Richie Havens will be appearing in a benefit concert for peace in the Middle East," Abbie said. "But tonight he will be sitting on Disingoff Street in the Cafe Casseta and he will be giving away fifty free tickets—*which the promoter is giving me right now*—to anyone who shows up and greets Richie with the words *'Isha Shalom.'* "

I almost burst out laughing on the air. There was no way my poor promoter could possibly object.

So on the following night while the tape was aired, there I was, sitting in the Cafe Casseta, talking with the owner, who had seen me perform "Shalom, Salaam Aleichem" live on Israeli TV, when Abbie's taped radio interview began to filter through a dozen nearby windows and shops. Within minutes, all the free tickets were gone, mostly to sixty-to-seventy-year-old men and women, the storekeepers, and shop owners of Disingoff Street. All but eight tickets that went to two carloads of young people who were listening on their car radios on their way through town. But all's well that ends well, as the added publicity Abbie generated certainly helped the promoter sell out the concert. They even had to turn away people at the door, which led the promoter to schedule an additional concert in the mountains in a small amphitheater (naturally carved in the rocks—outdoors and very green).

After the tickets were given away at the cafe, I began to feel the presence of a man sitting right behind me at the next table. We had been sitting back to back since I first arrived and now, with everyone else gone, we both turned slowly toward each other. And stopped. And stared. Right at each other. In complete silence.

If we were cartoon characters, there would have been question marks stamped on our foreheads.

I looked straight at this man and he looked straight at me

and it was as if we were looking in the mirror at our own reflections. Same angles to our faces. Same nose, same beards.

He was me. Only white.

I was him. Only black!

"You . . . you look . . . like *me,*" he said.

"No, you look like ME," I said.

"Who . . . who are you," he whispered in a very serious tone and I noticed that he was studying scriptures.

"I'm a musician. I play music and I'm here because of a peace song," I explained.

"You are lying to me," he said.

"No, I'm not," I said, and I explained further and he suddenly got very excited, but still deeply serious.

He asked if we could talk awhile. I had to go back to the hotel to do one more interview for a newspaper. So I invited him to come with me. We sat in the lobby with the reporter and he listened and learned more about how I happened to be in Israel.

After the interviewer left, we went to my room. He sat at the table near the window and said, "You will not believe this, Richie P. Havens, but I'm a musician too—I play cello."

My double was Roni Grundman, a virtuoso, a prodigy musical talent, the son of the famous Israeli architect who designed the world-famous Children's Memorial in Jerusalem. His mother was also an esteemed, internationally known artist. I was in the company of a very accomplished human being from a very accomplished family.

"I went to America once," my new friend said. "When I

got off the plane in New York, I took the taxi into the city and he left me off on a very busy street in front of a theater that said 'Fillmore.' "

My mind snapped listening to this, picturing the scene. Here was this poor guy, a classically trained musician, arriving in America for the first time without knowing much English, getting left off in the grungy East Village in front of rock 'n' roll's most outrageous showplace. Hundreds of young people mingling outside.

The taxi driver who had taken him from the airport had been talking to Roni all the way from the airport into Manhattan, but Roni understood very little. "I know where to take you," the taxi driver said.

The minute he stepped out of the cab onto the street he was approached by a man who came rushing out from the Fillmore. He could hardly be blamed if he thought that God had intervened on his behalf.

"Hey, do you want a job?" the man said. "Then come with me right now." The man grabbed him by the arm and picked up his suitcase.

"I didn't know where I was going or what was happening," my new friend continued. "He took me into the theater, stood me outside the men's room, and told me, 'If you see anybody come back here and start smoking—something, *any*thing—you come tell me.'

"I didn't know what he meant. But it didn't take long to find out. They did not fight or make problems, so I didn't have to say very much to my boss. I think he felt for me—being alone in America.

"It was a good, easy job," my new friend added. "I stayed for a month. I lived inside the Fillmore. I did not pay rent. I did not stay in hotel. I didn't have to go out from the Fillmore very often. *Everything* happened there and I saw you, Richie P. Havens. I remember now. But you didn't look like *me* then."

And I said, "This is so far out."

Nothing in this world is unconnected. *Nothing.*

"I saw you and I saw Jimi Hendrix," he whispered excitedly. "I saw *sooo* many great musicians. I saw you play, Richie Havens. I saw you play more than once." It was the first smile I saw on his face.

We stared at each other some more as a friendship was being born and Roni went on, "This is part of my problem now here in Israel. I go to America to see the great classic musicians in New York and instead I am coming home playing Jimi Hendrix on the cello. He was a master!

"No one in my family, no one in the orchestra wants to hear me anymore. Only my rock 'n' roll friends. I thought someday I would play Jimi Hendrix cello at the Fillmore, but I am married and have returned to my religion. I am only studying scriptures now."

We got to know each other more. We talked religion and philosophy and women and life and he was genuinely surprised that I had studied so many religions so seriously on my own, including some of the same Talmudic books he was studying under supervision of an esteemed Grand Rabbi in Svat, a town of deeply religious teachers.

I explained how I have spent much of my life trying to educate myself, searching for the truth of our roots. I told him I have always felt a burning need to know where we came from and what we're doing here. I told him how I have investigated and compared philosophical threads in the Old and New Testament, in Buddhism, and in the Koran, as well as the astrological writings of serious-minded students of the stars. He decided he should be going and as I walked him to the door he noticed my books on the dresser. The ones I read on planes and buses: the Zohar, the Talmud, the Koran, *Esoteric Astrology*.

He turned, looking me straight in the eye, and said again, *"Who are you,* Richie Havens?" with that question mark on his forehead. "I think I would like to take you to my home to meet my mother," he said. "I will see."

I was willing.

Two nights later, I was invited to dinner, but his mother left a note on the door, apologizing for her absence due to an illness of a close friend. She had gone to Jerusalem. Inside his home, my friend began to reveal to me layer by layer who his mother really was.

First he took me into a room where there were dozens of her drawings and paintings in huge bins.

The work was incredible.

Next he brought me into another room where he pulled out more of his mother's paintings. All were at least four and a half feet by six and a half feet and some were much, much larger.

What I saw was more than a collection of well-executed paintings. What I saw was the unique style and mind of his mother, the artist. Every painting evoked a clear emotion and revealed political or social commentary.

Every painting was constructed around a clothesline or telephone line with sheets or flags and/or banners hanging from clothes pins. Each hung object had a hat or bows painted on top and shoes tacked on to the bottom. And in the middle of the sheet or banner or flag was a face—painted to display an emotionally revealing expression. Deep and real . . . in conflict or joy . . . making an ironic political statement or comic point.

In some ways, her work resembled the political cartoons we see every day in newsprint, but this was done with such color and perspective that it went well beyond caricature. While I stared at each piece, I found myself thinking, *This is so strange, so vivid.* I couldn't take my eyes off them.

All these faces and all these expressions . . . they're talking to me, I thought. What a feeling. This was an artist who herself must be cut from a whole other cloth. And I did not know how right I was. My senses were right.

Roni was making tea while I looked at the paintings. When he handed me a cup, he sat down and said, "My mother cannot hear and she cannot speak . . . and she doesn't take to too many people. I must confess, I wanted to see her meet you. I wanted to see how she would react to you."

My friend invited me back to meet her in two days. After seeing her unique art, I understood that she spoke in facial expressions and many people understood her language through art.

I didn't need any coaxing.

When I did get to meet her, I didn't leave for four hours. We started *talking* together. Yes, *talking*. At the kitchen table. His mother was unable to hear and she spoke only in halting sounds and gestures. She could read my lips well, though, and we had no trouble at all understanding anything we each were trying to say.

She was an activist for peace in her country and did many things in her community to make that known.

Maybe I was in a better position to have this conversation than most. In fact, when I was sixteen, I had a girlfriend who could not speak or hear. And as a child growing up in Brooklyn, I remember going fishing many times with David McCrae's uncle, who was deaf. We had no problems communicating. He was a shoemaker and I worked with him for a couple of months.

My friend's mother spoke not one clear word. But the conversation flowed back and forth while my friend sat in a chair nearby, watching it all like a Ping-Pong game, amazed that we were able to understand *everything* passing between us.

It was one of the most remarkable conversations of my entire life. We talked about the issues facing the Middle East and the hope for a lasting peace. We spoke about the holocaust, about art, about music, about our families, and about the power of the mind to overcome all adversity. She was in her early forties and quite a beautiful person, and I can honestly say that I left her knowing more about the world and myself than I had known before I saw her drawings and paintings, before we communicated so intimately.

Before my final concert in Jerusalem, I was introduced to another Israeli, a man who would take me on an adventure I'll never forget. It began at a party that he hosted for all the faculty involved in the Peace Now students' organization and many of the students helping out with the concert were there.

While I was being introduced to this man, a very strange thing popped into my head. It was such a weird thing to be thinking. It was the movie *Close Encounters of the Third Kind,* which I had seen a week before leaving the United States to go to Israel.

"I'm looking for someone to talk to about a movie I just saw," I said.

To my surprise, my new acquaintance didn't laugh or look at me with a question mark on his forehead. He said simply, "You're a firstborn son, aren't you?" He had a deep Sabran accent.

"How did you know that?" I asked.

"I can see it on your face. I probably could tell everyone in this room if they were the first in their families." He had eighteen brothers and sisters and he was a firstborn himself. He also owned the best pizza shops in Israel—several of them.

"Richie," he continued, "sometimes we take trips into the desert to get away from the craziness in the city and we stop to visit ancient biblical places . . . We find it very calming . . . You might want to go with us—tomorrow morning. We can spend the day and be back for the concert." This was my first chance to see more of Jerusalem. I couldn't wait.

So the next morning—early—my strange new friend and I joined one of his friends and rode out into the desert. Early on, it was obvious that it was not a good day to see anything. Too much haze.

So my guide decided to shift direction, saying he had something else to show me. All the way down the road I'm talking about the movie I can't get out of my mind: Steven Spielberg's *Close Encounters of the Third Kind*. They told me it was coming to Israel in a week.

I raved how they had to see this film. I told them how the story line of the film was based on a collection of unexplained incidents in different parts of the world and might not be quite the fantasy it may seem to most. In fact, it may have a bit of truth to it.

Meanwhile, my new Israeli friend stopped the car on the road and said, "Here we are."

Right in front of me was the mountain that King Herod used as a summer palace when Jesus was alive—Herod's Mountain—a mountain that just happened to be shaped almost exactly like Devil's Tower, the Wyoming landing location for the alien spaceship in *Close Encounters*.

Here I had been thinking and talking about this remarkable movie that had not yet come to Israel and suddenly I was in the middle of the desert, looking right at a mirror image of the landsite that was nearly a living character in the film. I did not have to be reminded that I was doing this with a total stranger who seemed to read my mind. It dawned on me that if visitors from another world were ever going to land anywhere on this planet to make contact, it would of course be right here in the Holy Land. Where it all started. I certainly had plenty to think about on the flight back home—and for the rest of my life, in fact.

CHAPTER

the *aliens* among us

W hen I lived in a third-floor flat in the East Village years ago, a lady friend of mine, Stephanie Marco, exposed me to a handful of autistic kids she was working with. Every once in a while, Stephanie, an untrained nurse, would bring them over to visit.

Autism, as you may know, is a mystery to medical science. A biological anomaly, it seems to be a congenital condition linked to the way the nervous system is wired. Beyond that, science has no answer how it occurs or how to really deal with it. But there are plenty of caring people out there trying.

Some autistic kids do remarkable things, like reciting every phone number on a page after only a brief look. Yet the same kids may not be able—or willing—to spell their names or communicate coherently. Very few ever look at someone directly, although there is no doubt in my mind that many have an uncanny ability to focus on the world they live in while we fall all over ourselves to penetrate it.

A wide range of theories and new approaches have surfaced to try and bridge the communication gap, all of which should be explored carefully. But back in my East Village apartment, I stumbled upon a few things that are worth sharing.

Stephanie was talking to me about one of "her kids," an eight-year-old girl who spent a lot of her time running around the room in small circles.

"She's so hard to communicate with and she's never spoken," Stephanie said.

My first instinct was very clear.

"Probably you won't be able to talk with her until you get right into her world. Why don't you get down and run around with her in her little circle? My guess is that you might begin to reach her or understand what she's doing."

The following week Stephanie came by to tell me that she tried my suggestion. Everything had changed dramatically.

"I got in the circle and ran around with her," Stephanie said. "After a while, I began to feel as if I was *levitating*, almost as if my feet were leaving the ground."

"Well, you know what?" I told Stephanie. "In her reality, *her feet may NOT be* touching the ground." Stephanie nodded and shared another remarkable event that had occurred after their intimate day together. It seemed that part of the therapy was deprivation—to not feed the kids if they did not respond. Stephanie couldn't bear to do that and got caught feeding the little girl. So they took the little girl from her and gave her to another worker.

However, at a session with the other worker, the young girl said, "I want *Stephanie.*"

"According to her parents and doctors, that was the first time this girl had spoken a sentence in her life," Stephanie said. "The psychologist couldn't believe it."

All this left me thinking more about the little girl and what she enjoyed most in her life. I kept visualizing her crouched down as she ran around her circle as if she was chasing something. Suddenly I had a hunch.

"What is this girl's astrological sign?" I asked.

"Taurus."

I wasn't surprised.

"Taurus, *the Bull,*" I pointed out. "She's a little bull in the pen, running 'round and 'round. That's her world. When you get down with her, you join her in her private world. To know more about her, you definitely have to get into the circle with her."

Stephanie told me about another one of her autistic kids. A three-year-old boy who was always in the bathroom, trying to climb into the tub.

"Since he left the crib," Stephanie said, "he's wanted to crawl into the bathroom. Now that he can walk, he goes there and climbs into the tub until someone notices that he's missing. He's scaring the daylights out of his parents. They're worried he's going to slip and fall."

Stephanie said that whenever the boy makes it into the tub, he sits in it, looking straight ahead in a perfect lotus position, which I can personally attest is not easy to do.

RICHIE HAVENS

I love expressing myself through sculpture. This piece was inspired by
the breathtaking *Pietà* in Rome.

This puzzled me until Stephanie reminded me that the boy was so young and could not see over the sides of the tub when he sat in his favorite place.

"That's it!" I said.

"He's surrounded by pure white. He can't see over the side. All he sees is the white of the bathtub. He's in a pure natural state, staring into space with his feet locked in a primary lotus position. It's safe for him there and it probably is a place where he discovers things within himself that we can only *dream* about."

Stephanie reported about other autistic children and in each case there was a clue that helped to unravel some of the mystery—or at least put us both closer to understanding what was going on.

Three of her kids spoke coherently for the first time and one of them was a sixteen-year-old boy who couldn't eat his meals unless he drank milk from a baby bottle in Stephanie's lap. This boy presented another intriguing puzzle that was solved by his observant speech therapist.

During the first few minutes of regular speech therapy, the teacher began to notice that the boy would regularly walk to the front of the room and seemingly glance at a book she had on a table. He would lift it open, drop it, and continue to the front of the room.

After observing this behavior a few times, the speech therapist suspected that the boy might have been reading the material on the open book page in a few seconds. To test her theory, she prepared a series of multiple-choice questions related to an exposed page in her book. She then placed the quiz on the boy's desk before he arrived for the next session.

Do I have to tell you that without prompting of any kind, he sat down at his desk and correctly answered every question after taking his usual peek?

Like I said, these kids never look you straight in the eye, but it can be a big mistake to think they don't know what is going on around them.

"They can be reached," I said to Stephanie. "There has to be much more we're not seeing about them."

One other thing I observed about autism might be sheer coincidence, but it could be an important clue worth a closer look. In fact, I was surprised to learn that nearly all of the autistic children I encountered through Stephanie were sons and daughters of "professional parents": doctors married to teachers, or lawyers, or two teachers married to each other. And beyond that, there also seemed to be a relationship between the lifestyles of the parents and their kids.

The girl who ran around in a circle was expressing herself in a very physical way, but her parents were both scholars—teachers, in fact—who were not inclined toward sports or physical expressions. The boy who sat silently in the white bathtub was the son of physically active parents and he expressed himself through his mental connection to his world. The sixteen-year-old who intuitively *absorbed* the open book on his speech therapist's desk had parents who were involved in action-oriented professions. And so on.

In other words, each child tended to connect to his or her

world in a way that was almost directly opposite to the intense skills or personality traits of their parents! While these were just my "unscientific" observations, I can only suggest that the medical community should check the ideas out themselves.

Throughout my life—from my teenage years in Bed-Stuy, my time in Greenwich Village, my travels, my role as a parent and grandparent (five times over), and my working experience with the North Wind Undersea Institute and the Natural Guard—I have seen too many children oversupervised, poorly educated, and badly underestimated for their intelligence and personal initiative.

This is partly due, I think, to several misunderstandings about the way children really grow up and the incredible speed with which the world continues to change so dramatically as we approach the millennium.

Anyone looking at history knows that our civilization has been moving at the speed of light during the last 100 years. Even if we ignore diet cola, hula hoops, and the ridiculous aluminum baseball bat, we can cite fuel-injected automobiles; manned flight, jet flight, and space flight; digital photography, TV and radio telescopes; nuclear energy; the sexual revolution; the Internet; lasers; and the advancing computer sciences— just to name some of the most obvious technological and social changes.

Among other things, the sheer speed of these changes has led me to believe that we badly underestimate the length of *generation gaps* in our society. Instead of the usual twenty-to-twenty-five-year period from childhood to mother- or fatherhood that previously characterized gaps between the generations, it is my view that such gaps now occur far more frequently. Actually, it seems absurd to look at generations in twenty-year blocks. In our world—where highly popular trends disappear in weeks and new technologies are invented every six months—cultural changes occur so frequently that if you and your sister were born as little as three years apart, there is likely to be a gap between what each of you see and understand.

That is a true gap between two different generations, and it is time parents and teachers come to grips with it.

Consider this. Just nine years after I was born, a brand-new generation came along that missed all of the 1940s.

Three years after Richard Nixon was elected in 1968, a whole generation was born that did not experience the Vietnam War, the assassinations of President John Kennedy, Robert Kennedy, and Martin Luther King, Jr. It's pretty hard for me to believe that those traumas did not have major impact on the world our children were born into. From personal experience, I can tell you that each of those assassinations had a profound effect on me personally—as a young man learning my art and gaining my adulthood in Greenwich Village. And they had enormous impact on everybody I have ever met.

We, the children born in the early 1940s, and the 'baby boomers' born immediately after World War II, grew up with our parents earning more money than their parents had ever seen. We grew up with more mobility and restlessness than any prior generation since the early colonists came to America in the 1700s.

Our restlessness was expressed through James Dean, rhythm and blues, Elvis Presley, and the beginnings of the civil rights movement in the South. Many of us were first-generation Americans who grew up somewhat defiant of our parents. Our music was rebellious and full of challenges to all that had gone before it. The songs we sang and the plays and books we wrote could not remain silent.

We watched and participated in all of this before we raised our own children into the 1980s and 1990s, and we helped push all the changes along. That's who we were, that's who we are. And when we stop and assess our place in history, I wonder how many of us will notice that our youth continue to recreate the world every few years in their own vision. I wonder how many of us will really take seriously the underlying message in Bob Dylan's great anthem "The Times They Are a-Changin'." The simple truth is that we are finding out that each new generation has less time to lead the parade.

Today's kids regularly test limits and experiment with anything new. Many believe they don't have to do anything anybody tells them. So what! That's exactly how I felt as far back as I can remember, even when our parents made us pay with our hides when we stepped over the line. And isn't it interesting that the relaxation of parental strictness in the 1970s and 1980s has led to an age in which there is even more rebellion in our youth than before. So what! Today's rebellion is leading toward many positive changes in our society, with more to come.

Consider that millions of young people throughout the world have no fear of tackling many issues we adults were so slow to address. Or that today's youth are more interested in environmental issues, racial and sexual issues, issues that were very uncomfortable to our parents and grandparents. This is what I have seen in South Africa, Israel, Germany, and the streets of New York, Los Angeles, and 100 American cities and towns. This is what I experienced regularly working with kids at the North Wind Undersea Institute and the Natural Guard.

By the beginning of the next millennium, maybe we will finally realize that our kids deserve to have unencumbered access to more sophisticated information and more tools (such as the computer) to connect the dots between different cultures. At the bottom line, they deserve more opportunities to develop their *own* ideas.

While parenting today is far from an easy job in a complex world, we must avoid falling into the trap of those who came before us and not raise our kids simply to *follow leaders and watch their parking meters.*

All of us have heard countless politicians say that our children are our future, but they are only half-right. The other half of this reality is that our future is *now.* And there may be even another way to look at it . . . Sometimes I think people are right to believe there really are *aliens* among us. In fact, I know they are right—except for one thing. The aliens among us are *not* from outer space.

The aliens *among us are our kids.*

And if we really know what's good for us, we'd better pay attention to what they are saying. Like the aliens in science fiction stories, *they are getting ready to take over the world.* That is our legacy—and it's the best thing that could happen to ensure our own survival.

the truth about drugs

When I watched my good friend Kenny Schneider lose all control over his life back in Brooklyn, I didn't need another thing to convince me that taking hard drugs was a one-way ticket to hell.

Still, after observing lots of people smoke marijuana with nothing approaching that kind of trauma, I knew there was something else going on that I had to check out. My curiosity always has been a powerful force in my life.

The first time I smoked a joint I was sixteen. I was on a rooftop with friends in Brooklyn and I didn't feel a thing. I told them they were nuts and continued on with my life.

Three years later at a wedding, I smoked grass again and listened to the great Indian musician Ravi Shankar play sitar for the first time and really felt what it was like. Grass had an almost hypnotic effect. It mellowed me and simultaneously intensified my senses.

I never touched it again until several years later in the Village.

All the propaganda that said grass was habit-forming or that it was a trapdoor to hard drugs was as false as so many other lies being told to my generation. Lies about the dangers of masturbation. Supposedly, it caused *blindness* . . . Yeah, right! Lies about the so-called *evils* of rock 'n' roll, or the absurd single-bullet theory of the Kennedy assassination, or the reasons for the Vietnam War, or the benign wonders of a few beers at the local pub.

I knew one thing for sure. No one I saw get high on marijuana ever got into a violent rage. And I sure couldn't say the same about a whole lot of drinkers at the neighborhood bar. Imagine how many billions of dollars the government makes from the taxes on bottles of Scotch and cigarette packs.

Before "clean" grass was corrupted and "stretched" with potent additives or dirty fillers on the street, it was a far, far better alternative to alcohol. Unlike booze, which has contributed to millions of auto deaths and acts of domestic violence, grass was the most lied-about substance my generation ever encountered. Not only was it something that did not numb the senses or cause wild mood swings, it had gentle mind-expanding properties. It was a nonviolent drug, a communal drug. And besides, it even cured my sinus headaches, my post-nasal drip, and earaches that I suffered all of my life. Seriously. In my case, it did.

I know it is controversial for me to be speaking positively about such a drug—any *drug*. But I believe that one of the key reasons why we have major drug problems in America is how much lying has gone on about them. For instance, instead of trying to scare us half to death about grass in the sixties, I'm convinced that sharing the truth about its real properties would have muted much of the excessive use and abuse that stemmed from kids reacting to the lies with rebellion—their only weapon of survival.

Isn't that the way it works?

Adults lie to their kids about this or that and the kids immediately try the *big bad thing* for themselves to see if it is true what they say about it. Next thing you know, the kids see the lie for what it is and do it again. More important, the same kids instantly lose respect for the adults who misled them.

During the sixties, new drugs started appearing in the Village and other American cities. Psychedelic drugs. Drugs that were not killers like heroin or addictive like cocaine. Drugs that were artificially created in the laboratory, drugs with powerful mind-altering, mind-expanding properties. It all seemed a natural reaction to the times. The world was becoming smaller and moving at a superfast pace. The new psychedelic drugs played into that pace and also slowed things down for those searching more intensely for their spiritual roots or a route out of society's constant pressures.

While grass—at least clean grass and homegrown grass— was relatively harmless, LSD was not a benign drug, or a party drug, or even a drug for escape. It was far stronger, far more complicated, with a big plus and minus. Where naturally grown drugs like mescaline and peyote had been cultivated for spiritual and hallucinatory rituals by Native Americans for hundreds of years, LSD was a relatively new chemical combination with equally powerful properties. And it came to us through CIA experiments, which we paid for, by the way, with our taxes.

Two of my best Village friends, Marcellus and Dino Valenti, were the first people I knew who were into LSD. Both seemed aware of its potency, both used it sparingly, mostly in each other's presence—for self-exploration and deep personal discovery.

"This is powerful stuff," they often said. "But you can learn a lot about yourself and you can see things in the natural world that you miss every day."

Dino and Marcellus reported seeing trees expand and contract as if they were breathing and they watched blades of grass grow, millimeter by millimeter.

Beyond the intensity of their LSD experiences, I learned a lot about the drug by trying it twice and watching and talking to dozens upon dozens of people who were into it.

Passive LSD users regularly experienced wild hallucinations that stretched the boundaries of reality beyond recognition. Aggressive or creatively curious people, like Marcellus and Dino, usually remained grounded in reality and found their senses intensified without hallucinations. While persons who hallucinated regularly conjured up things that were physically impossible, people like Marcellus and Dino never saw anything like a tree or a car flying over their next-door neighbor's house.

In most cases, I could predict which person on LSD would lose their anchor to reality and which ones, like Marcellus and Dino, would see the natural world with great intensity or be open to deep personal discoveries. Those who were tagging along with friends or seemed unwilling to do things on their own were usually the ones who tripped into the wildest hallucinations, replacing, I guess, the absence of their own individual vision of the world around them. People who came to the drug seeking an introspective adventure—or a spiritual experiment into the unknown—usually saw new aspects of the real world. Perhaps even the hairs on the back of their hands as if they were looking through microscopic eyes.

In other words, there were many LSD users who did not turn the natural world upside down or inside out; they just saw it in sharper focus or more intensely. Still, I was not moved by the experiences to pursue taking it beyond my two trips. While I too had introspective experiences and felt as if I had conquered some of my own demons, I honestly did not like the long hours it took to return to so-called "normal." Ten hours was way too long for me to place myself into a semistate of suspended animation. And besides, grass was good enough for me.

Still, I'm convinced that the way our society, the government, and the press reflexively lumped acid and grass together with viciously addictive drugs like heroin and cocaine contributed enormously to the drug problem in our streets.

Grass had been around for a long time and was being used and abused by a relatively small percentage of people who were turned on to it. Heroin also had been around for a long time, but had been under relative control in the sixties, with many addicts gaining legal access to supposedly safer drugs such as methadone through community-sponsored programs. But when society decided to crack down against young people with their taboo grass and acid, organized gangs seized the opportunity to flood the streets with harder drugs, including cocaine and its more dangerous cousin, crack cocaine.

Relatively expensive cocaine zoomed in popularity among affluent thrill seekers and the poorly informed. Dirt-cheap and extremely dangerous crack took hold in our poorest neighborhoods.

Where heroin use was up slightly as part of the trend, coke—and particularly crack—became a way out. An escape from the pressures of the real world. A social instrument shared among disenfranchised peoples who had more money than hope—or none of either.

Whatever drug filled the hole or the emptiness became the drug of choice. That is, it seems to me, the root of all addiction. The person seeking out his addiction in the first place is emotionally empty in some area, maybe totally. He wants to be filled by the feeling the drug generates. All the time. Any feeling.

If the addiction is tobacco, the best way to stop smoking is to replace the feeling with something equally stimulating or creative. Maybe the hands that light and hold the cigarette should write or draw. The mouth that holds and draws smoke into the lungs doesn't have to take in more food, but that does happen to a lot of people in the early stages of trying to quit. Because it is the hand that does it all. Move the cigarettes to your lips; open the fridge and put the food in your mouth.

It is sad, but most of the people who deal in the legality and criminality of drugs rarely see the addictive personality as a real human being with a deep psychological problem. Instead, they see a set of reactions; they see that person acting out in their society, which triggers a one-way reaction: Chain them up. Label them incorrigible, hopeless, or both. Put them away. Keep them from contact with the rest of the world. Bury them under the rug. And make money on them at the same time. How many own stock in private prisons and who are you?

Don't get me wrong. I'm a firm believer in self-help. Self-help is the guiding principle for recovery, but at the same time we can do better—a whole lot better—as a connected society. More of us must go into the worst of neighborhoods and truly invest more human energy and business capital to improve local schools and alleviate the conditions too many people are forced to cope with every day. Until we do that through our collective will, we will go on building more jails, throwing away more people who never will leave us anyway. Some, the ones we probably have ignored the most, will fulfill our lowest expectations and tear up our world limb from limb.

It's an old story, one we keep repeating, no matter how many times we pay the consequences.

In the sixties we knew that LSD was far more potent and unpredictable than grass. We knew that a small percentage of

LSD users definitely wound up in some pretty bad places. Such *bad trips,* though, were very important in the scheme of things, but no one was trying to understand what was going on.

The media laughed at Timothy Leary when he started talking about his LSD experiments at Harvard. Bad trips? There was an appalling lack of serious examination into the worst of them by the psychological community. And it was equally appalling that every incident was sensationalized and exploited in the media.

From what I saw up close, the people who had bad trips were troubled individuals, acting out all over the place before they ever took a psychedelic drug. Yet in the end, the inevitable breakdown was blamed directly on the drug. That's not good enough . . . Whatever LSD's true properties and dangers, nobody really seemed ready to discover them.

From what I personally saw, an acid trip could be positive and enlightening, yet completely different for each person. Misuse and potential abuse were a function of the attitudes and problems brought to the experience by the user. And there were real dangers in the dosage and purity of it.

Those issues convinced me that society has to be very careful that it does not lie about LSD or any drug when the next wave of interest or new drug comes to the fore.

At the bottom line, I believe controlled doses of LSD should be made available under controlled conditions to responsible adults who wish to investigate themselves with it. Why not? It is, after all, a potential tool for self-discovery, not an addictive killer.

RICHIE HAVENS

What about grass? Should it be legalized? What about crack cocaine and other modern variations of drugs being used by street gangs to control territories and undermine neighborhoods in hundreds of cities and towns?

Should any of these drugs be legal?

In my judgment, it is probably too late in the history of drug use in America to open a door that should have been opened forty years ago. If mind-altering drugs had been made legal in the 1950s and early 1960s, if people had been given the correct information about them, if traffic in such drugs had not been made into a lucrative contraband business, if our own government did not act as if it had a vested interest in keeping the trade alive, if we as a society were truly committed to teaching our children the truth about everything, we would have little to fear from drugs and we would not be in the fix we are in now.

But the opportunity was lost; the horse has left the barn. It is no longer practical to legalize drugs, at least not unilaterally.

What I would like to see is very simple and constructive.

What I would like to see is what I have been saying here: *an end to the hypocrisy.*

First and foremost, any marijuana use prescribed by doctors for medicinal purposes should be legal without question. The fact that this is not so after so much evidence has been compiled proving its medicinal and painkilling benefits to very ill patients is an appalling indictment of the rigid thinking that has clouded this issue for decades.

Second, wouldn't it make sense to relax the legal restrictions on grass by permitting anyone to grow a single plant for his or her own use in his own home or apartment without fear of breaking any law? Shouldn't Constitutional guarantees of freedom and privacy be in play here? Wouldn't it be better to worry about people selling or distributing to minors or conducting serious trade in grass, rather than criminalize social users, or people otherwise behaving in a legal manner?

What is it that we are trying to protect here?

Another thing I would like to see is the destruction of all captured contraband presently held by government officials and border police. It may surprise you to learn that thousands of tons of confiscated drugs—from grass to coke to heroin—are not destroyed each year. Given that, would you be surprised to learn that many tons of seized crack cocaine and other hard drugs regularly disappear from police and government depots every year only to wind up back on the street. Do we want to crack down on illegal *hard drugs* or not?

Do we want to tell the truth about which drugs are killers, which ones are addictive, and which ones are less harmful than alcohol? Or do we simply want to throw more people in our jails to pay lip service to rehabilitation and make believe we did the right thing. Oh, by the way, what are you drinking in front of your kids tonight?

back to the future

To me Woodstock is not just a time or place or a terrific three-day concert in 1969 that attracted hundreds of thousands of people. It is not the mud baths people took in the rain or the good movie that showed the world how so many young people from all generations and walks of life could get along together. We were already getting along together.

What happened on Max Yasgur's farm in Bethel, New York, went beyond all of those things. Woodstock was shared around the world by people who weren't even there.

Maybe none of us really appreciated the true historical significance of Woodstock while it was coming together, but we could feel it on the tip of our tongues. We were the first global-minded generation. The first who could travel easily from continent to continent and witness in our living rooms events halfway around the world. Our music was different, challenging, electrifying, a blend of different cultures. And many of our songs dared to raise questions about human rights and the point of war in a nuclear world.

The Dylan song was right: The times really were a-changin', and Woodstock was a dramatic demonstration that young people were more than ready.

Think about it. We gathered together on a hillside in New York State at a time when the world was turning upside down. The Soviet Union was rattling its sabers in Eastern Europe, the Middle East was on fire as it had been for decades, the Vietnam War was in full swing, and our newly elected President—"Tricky Dick" Nixon—was ignoring the hundreds of thousands of people protesting against it in the streets.

During this gut-wrenching but impressive decade, we had already witnessed the assassination of a beloved President; the assassination of a beloved black leader who *peacefully* forced America to confront its racism for the first time; and the assassination of a potential president, Robert Kennedy, brother of the slain leader we had barely time to mourn. We could have been excused if we felt overloaded and actually did drop out as the press often stated.

Indeed, the press persistently radicalized our generation as the "great unwashed" or as "hippies" and "draft dodgers." Supposedly, we had nothing important to say, nothing on our minds other than sex, drugs, and rock 'n' roll.

The big-city newspapers that so casually suggested riots were likely to happen at Woodstock had to eat their words by the end of the weekend. The large numbers who invaded the surrounding hillside were not there to trash a town; they were there to enjoy a good show and, in a subliminal way, to make a powerful statement: "This is our world too and we know a little bit more than you all think about how to handle ourselves. You can put us down, but we're here and you can't take us lightly."

Little did I realize that I would find thousands of people around the world sharing those feelings; so many said they felt they too had been at the Aquarian Music and Arts Fair along with all the people who actually were there. Little did I know that in South Africa twenty-nine-years later I would be asked to sing "Freedom" and "Handsome Johnny" by college students and guitarists who were not even born in 1969.

In every country and every part of America, I have continued to meet people who ask me questions and share their convictions about the Woodstock experience. What it means to them. What it represents.

- "We saw so many Americans singing songs from so many cultures. We felt our culture was there too."
- "Conditions were not very good there, but you all seemed so happy and lived so peacefully."
- "The music reached our hearts and our minds."
- "We saw brotherhood in Woodstock. Why can't there be more of that everywhere?

There *was* brotherhood in Woodstock and the feeling transcended the event that took place in a given time and place.

For all of us who were there and those who tuned in to it from afar, Woodstock was and has remained a worldwide community of kindred spirits, a community of young and old who saw or heard what was happening and have come to identify with it on many levels.

The music was one level, clearly exposing new talents to the world, as so few who performed were well known to the public before the event.

It was Crosby, Stills, and Nash's first gig on their debut tour. Peter Townshend and the Who may have been among the few acts people knew, but they became international megastars after appearing there. Sly and the Family Stone—one of the first racially integrated rock groups—made a strong impression playing "I Want to Take You Higher" and "Dance to the Music" after a marginal West Coast public career.

When people at the University of Indiana asked me the night after my Woodstock appearance what really happened back in Bethel, I told them I had come away from the event feeling that something very good had happened for *us*—not just young people, but for *all* people. I told them that I was hopeful that other Americans would see their sons and daughters differently and that people in other nations also would understand that there were large numbers of Americans trying to get along, doing good things together.

I had already been to Europe twice in the 1960s and almost every other question and comment I got over there was about the way black people were being treated here. There was harsh criticism and outright disbelief, which we all shared. Yet, I didn't carry any depressed feelings about that with me back then and I don't carry any now. That's not my nature.

I carry hopeful feelings, knowing that the world we live in is a work in progress, and the 1960s was a crucial turning point when people were beginning to wake up. Woodstock was one way to help people wake up, and we're still waking up. Anything that would help us I was willing to do.

The "Woodstock community" certainly was the motivating essence for those who wrote songs and talked about it all around the globe and back again. It was the most meaningful souvenir taken away from the place. And I have to say that the place itself was partly the driving force behind all of these feelings.

This I know to be true because every time I have returned to the site I have felt something. In its own way, Max Yasgur's old farm seems like holy ground.

During the summer of 1998, the twenty-ninth anniversary of the Woodstock Festival was held on the exact location, with a stage planted right on the spot where it all began in 1969. I can tell you that despite the concert promoter's attempts to make a commercial score and bypass the spiritual essence of the place, it still felt almost sacred to be there.

We were back on the scene where America changed some of its perceptions about young people, where hundreds of thousands of the "great unwashed" managed to live peaceably in a three-day community of music, peace, and mud.

The idealism of our youth had been replaced by the trials of parenthood and other trappings of adulthood. The hippies of 1969 were now schoolteachers, lawyers, accountants, doctors, truck drivers, and even grandparents. I too returned as a grandparent of five, and with several lifetimes of experiences, as you've read. But here we were, back on the original Woodstock site, touching base with the uniqueness of this very special natural arena.

For me, A Day in the Garden—the first commercial concert on the Yasgur farm since 1969—was an exciting emotional trip. The crowds, much larger than the producers announced (18,000 Friday, 26,000 Saturday, and 30,000 Sunday), brought back vivid memories of my helicopter flights in and out of the place twenty-nine years earlier.

The music was good—very good—all the way through. Yet, the goings on behind the scenes bothered me a lot. Especially when I reflect on the wonderful opportunity that exists for someone of means and good intentions to build upon the essence of the Woodstock experience on every level.

Long before anyone knew about A Day in the Garden, I got a call from Alan Gerry, whose multibillion-dollar company—CVI Cable—now owns the Yasgur farm.

Gerry knew little about the music of the original Woodstock, but his daughter Robyn had convinced him to buy the land because she had such positive memories of the 1969 festival. After a thorough financial investigation, Gerry not only bought the land but pledged his resources to build something important there—perhaps a permanent site for music and the arts, a site that would be true to the Woodstock tradition while helping the Sullivan County economy.

RICHIE HAVENS

Early in 1998, Gerry called me up to the site to ask for my counsel. I told him all I knew about the place, about the original festival, the way people such as Melanie and so many others had come back to "Woodstock" many times to keep the flame alive while rekindling the spirit for new generations.

I told him there are few musical venues in the world to match the natural comfort of this place or its suitability for outdoor staging. I told him that many of us who had played on that stage would support his efforts, so long as he respected the essence of the original Woodstock.

I told him the Woodstock idea still had considerable resonance with people all over the world, more than most promoters understood, and that he had a unique opportunity to build upon a great accomplishment that had been waiting for someone like him.

Gerry said he wanted to do two things. "I want to work with the people of Sullivan County to make sure that the community as a whole benefits from whatever we decide to do, and I want to make a permanent center for music here. But I want to consult with you, Richie, and other original performers. You can help guide us toward a better Woodstock, rather than one that will go against the feelings of those who remember what happened here."

True to his word, Gerry worked with the townspeople on many fronts, allaying their fears. Permits for a three-day anniversary concert were obtained, limiting the crowd to 30,000 per day. Sleeping on the site or in the parking lot would not be allowed. Traffic would be manageable. Security was tight—

maybe too tight—with four separate firms hired to look into packages and bags for food containers, cameras, booze, and dope. Some of this was excessive, but understandable given the town's skittish feelings about playing host to so many people again. It also was clear that there would be no drug party on the Yasgur hillside.

Gerry told the promoter he hired—Danny Socoloff of Granite Productions in Las Vegas—to call me first before he put the show together. I told Socoloff that this was not just another concert hall. This was not Madison Square Garden or Wolf Trap or the Hollywood Bowl. This did not have to be a "name thing," a place where expensive headliners are needed to attract attention.

"People will come to this site to see performers who were part of the original Woodstock Festival, mixed in with high-quality, little-known talents who deserve to be exposed to larger audiences," I said.

I didn't tell him who should be there; that was not my place. But I did give him a list of people he should consider inviting, including a handful of the original Woodstock performers and several underexposed talents who would light up the place, just like so many of the original performers did in 1969.

"People come to this site in the spirit of pilgrimage every year, " I told him. "The place will draw people. They'll come for the connection to the Woodstock idea and the Woodstock community. A well-planned commercial concert that is true to the spirit of this place will do as well as any high-priced concert."

I tried to impress upon him that the Yasgur farm in Bethel is one of those special places where a variation of that phrase from the baseball fantasy movie *Field of Dreams* is absolutely true: "Build it [right] and they will come."

All of this reflected the ideas Gerry and I discussed months before A Day in the Garden was proposed. But it was worlds apart from the approach Socoloff put into play.

Instead of a blend between original Woodstock regulars and relatively unknown but great talents, Socoloff called months later to tell me, "Guess who we got? *Bob Dylan* and *Joni Mitchell*." My reaction was silent, but the voice inside me was wondering where his head was at.

Dylan and Joni Mitchell? I thought. *This isn't a name thing. Why would anyone spend so much money when they didn't need to? Especially when the audience is being limited to thirty thousand a day?*

That's what I said silently to myself. What I said to him aloud was: "Well, they weren't there in '69, but people will come to see them."

A few weeks later, I learned that Dylan wasn't going to make it after all and Socoloff had cut a whole new deal with the management group that represents Stevie Nicks and Don Henley to bring them in for about half a million dollars apiece.

Half a million apiece!?!

At least that's what the manager of one of the performers

told me. And two days later, it was confirmed in *Performances* magazine, a highly reliable source for that kind of detail.

By the time Socoloff got through with his bookings, he had at least $2 million at risk on Nicks, Henley, Mitchell, Lou Reed, and Pete Townshend, plus some more on the Sunday show that featured well-known alternative rock performers.

This new Woodstock venture was supposed to be different. A commercial venture with high regard for the Woodstock spirit, launched on the site of the original festival. We, the artists, were to be included in the planning. We were going to be treated with respect.

I could not believe it when I learned that Donovan was guaranteed so much less than a fair sum that he would barely make expenses and that the promoter was not even going to invite Melanie until a fuss was raised about her absence. A Woodstock without Melanie, who had appeared many years on the site for free, would not be at Woodstock at all.

This was not a case of misplaced idealism. I had no illusions about any of this. People will always try to make money from Woodstock. But the way I see it, everybody's fees should have been close to the same. That's what a festival is about. Nobody is a "star." Nobody gets a huge fee at the expense of others in the cast. Everybody is part of the whole and there is a sense of community among the performers as much as there is in the audience. A long time ago, I learned a valuable lesson about the work I do. The stage does not belong to the *ringmasters* and promoters who "own" the rights to a momentary event any more than it belongs to the performers who step upon it.

The stage belongs to the audience.

By their very presence, they permit the magic that occurs there. If people are not present to watch and listen and respond, the most lavish or well-appointed venue in the world will be devoid of any life or fire. We who entertain must respect that fact or give up the effort to be allowed onto that hallowed platform.

Too often, promoters are unable to resist taking credit for a successful outcome when the event reaches heights they never could have imagined—heights way beyond their projected bottom line. Such was the case for the original Bethel event we call Woodstock and the recent 1998 event, A Day in the Garden. In both instances, it was the audience and the interplay with the performers that made each occasion a truly lasting and inspired gathering. And no matter how often this dynamic is demonstrated in arenas around the world, few promoters will acknowledge that it is this very magic that is responsible for their biggest profits.

While I spent most of the time at A Day in the Garden behind the stage as the "Webcast" host, I could not help but feel that *the event itself was the Master Player.*

A few weeks before A Day in the Garden was to occur a call to Alan Gerry's right-hand man, Darrell Supac, revealed that nobody in the Gerry organization had any idea what was going down. Supac seemed genuinely annoyed.

"This is all wrong, Richie," Supac said. A few days later,

Alan Gerry also called to let me know that much had occurred without his knowledge. Gerry now was fully aware that the Woodstock site had even more potential than his daughter Robyn first suggested and he was talking openly with county politicians and businessmen about using the Yasgur farm for a series of concerts on summer weekends. He was even consulting Michael Lang—one of the promoters of the original Woodstock—about a possible thirtieth anniversary weekend in 1999. Gerry did not want this twenty-ninth anniversary event—his first commercial venture on the site—to blow up in his face.

"We can change some things in time," Gerry said. "But would you play ball with us this year? We won't let this happen for the thirtieth anniversary next year."

Within days, ticket prices were slashed from the ridiculously high seventy dollars per day to a two-for-one deal. Eventually, the tab came down to a straight thirty-five dollars per day per ticket. Yet, all this could have been avoided. Without fear of contradiction, I know we could have put together a strong bill of performers for three days that would have attracted as much interest for less than half a million dollars for the whole weekend.

Beyond the last-minute changes, including some to my own contract, I went "back to the garden" for one principal reason: Gerry's personal commitment to me that he would not make the same mistakes with the larger-scale thirtieth anniversary festival in 1999. Gerry, an effective businessman, seemed to be learning quickly that a successful venture on that site would have to remain faithful to the concept born in 1969.

In 1994, the twenty-fifth reunion of the Woodstock Festival that Lang put on in Saugerties, New York—after he lost a bid to put one on in Bethel—was so commercial, so alien to the original concept that it fell flat on its face. And when the promoter who won the Bethel bid suddenly bailed out from the proposed event with three days to go, some of us took up the slack to set things right.

I made sure the sound and lights were there. My friend Bernie Fox brought tons of equipment a long way to the farm. What we had was a spontaneous, *free* music festival and a true reunion for more than eight thousand people and the many performers who learned about it through word of mouth. This was far from the first time people had journeyed to Bethel on August 15, 16, and 17 to touch base with the original event.

Every year there has been some sort of free musical gathering on or near the site.

In 1989, the twentieth anniversary of Woodstock was celebrated in a manner that was very much in tune with the original event. It was not on the site, but it did have several of the original festival performers, including John Sebastian, Melanie, Country Joe, myself, and others who joined along the way. I helped organize it. When we were unable to get permission to use the farm for an event, we took to the road and stopped in more than two dozen towns and villages, singing our way from New York to California throughout the summer.

We didn't do this to make big profits (and that was just as

well—after our traveling business partner ran off with the money). We were on the road for different reasons. We were keeping faith with the Woodstock community, taking it to the people—something we might do again.

This time, in 1998, when I stepped out onto the Bethel stage again—twenty-nine years after opening the original event—I still could feel the connection we all had when we struggled to be heard the first time around. I really could. It was the same energy that pervaded the atmosphere so many years ago. It embraced us all. We were indeed "back in the garden." Our garden.

Seeing the people in the crowd, hearing the music, I knew things were going to be discovered and made clear again. We still were family—even more so. Those of us old enough to remember the first event were veterans of the struggle that had produced major changes in the world and in ourselves. Those there for the first time could sense the direct link this place had to battles we had fought and won. What I was witnessing in the eyes of so many people was a true testament to our becoming more of ourselves.

I felt the energy of the crowd hit me and I was empowered once again to speak my mind through the songs I sang, as I have on so many stages since our first gathering. I can't say that I felt a heck of a lot of difference in the battles we still have to fight, but I could feel there are plenty of us who have remained strong enough to hold the line. We continue to live what we fought for.

I was strongly moved by the numbers of young people

Onstage at a Day in the Garden, 1998. *(Photo by Steve Davidowitz)*

who seemed to be looking for their connection to the mirage of the past, only to find out, with some surprise, that it was still there in Bethel. In so many young eyes I saw the same good vibrations that I saw in the people around them who had experienced the original event. I am convinced that many of these young people felt the depth with which we embraced our experience. They were there now, finding their own experience.

This festival wasn't anywhere near as big as the original Bethel event—at least not in live attendance. But through the worldwide Internet broadcast, those taking part this time were many hundreds of thousands stronger than the huge crowd that made history in 1969.

The World Wide Web didn't exist back then. Now it was making it possible to broadcast the event live to all who wished to tune in from the convenience of their own home or from any computer with a modem. More than a million people around the world did so.

In my heart, I believe it was our tenacity to stay connected as a generation that became the driving creative force behind the emergence of the fantastic communication technology we now utilize to reach across the globe in our daily lives. I believe the same global connection fostered the actual high-tech Bethel/Internet stage we were all playing upon this time around.

Peter Townshend gave his heart and soul to the days he spent in the garden. So did Melanie—and her three kids who played with her—and Ten Years After, who felt the connection to the original festival all over again. Joni and Donovan definitely were glad to touch base with the magic. You could feel it in their performances.

Now that a major corporation is behind the site's future, we can only hope that the lessons of the recent past will guide future endeavors. If, as we approach the millenium, there is a sincere effort to build a permanent center for music on the original site, it is vital that Alan Gerry's commitment to the artists, to the site, and to the townspeople should be the operating principle for everything that develops.

At the bottom line, if the people with the money and the political clout do not do right by future Woodstock festivals, I personally will make sure that there will be one somewhere on this Earth that lives up to the legacy of the original. As I said before leaving the stage after singing "Freedom" again in 1998, "This place belongs to us—forever."

they really can't hide us anymore

I went to South Africa in the fall of 1997 on the invitation of David Marx, a musician who actually was the man who set my microphones on the Woodstock stage in 1969. David was visiting from South Africa that year and got a job with Handley, the sound company that had been hired by Michael Lang to work the Woodstock Festival. When he went back to South Africa, David formed one of his country's first mixed bands. He got in a lot of political trouble for that and faced physical danger on his gigs and elsewhere until South Africa shed apartheid in the wave of social and political changes inspired by Nelson Mandela.

After a return visit to Woodstock in the summer of '97, David made connections to a California-based promoter from Durban, who in turn made other arrangements with other promoters in Johannesburg. It was more than a chance to travel to one of the few foreign lands I had not visited, a land connected to my great-great-grandparents' roots. As a musician, I was looking forward to the incredible music of South Africa and to meet and be with people who had only recently entered a new phase of their political and social existence.

In Johannesburg, I actually felt like the hero in Mark Twain's *A Connecticut Yankee in King Arthur's Court.* A visitor in time, going back to his root culture. Musically and otherwise. I did four concerts in three major South African cities, plus many interviews for various media and press, all of them curious about the Woodstock experience and music of the Western world.

I saw more interracial couples walking the streets in two weeks than I usually see in two months in New York or D.C. I saw men with cell phones everywhere and street police and tribal guards who carried military weapons with the same nonchalance as you or I might carry a shopping bag from the supermarket. Yet, I saw nobody hassled by the police, no one refused service at a lunch counter, no negative racial attitudes expressed in any social encounter as opportunities continue to be created for all in daily commerce.

I met people who were struggling with the rapid changes in their society, but they were hopeful people, people who smiled a lot and were beginning to see changes in their lives from the evils of apartheid and a tribal-based society to one with democratic possibilities. There was hope in the air. Everywhere.

I did many workshops and seminars. Guitar playing and singing workshops with guest musicians from the local town

This piece was scanned into my computer and printed from there.
New technology is opening up a world of possibilities for everyone.

I was in, both white and black musicians among the partici-
pants and the audience.

Michael Jackson was also in South Africa, playing the same
major cities as I did, usually on the same days or the day before
or after. In one town they dedicated a statue in his honor
and the front pages of the local newspapers were filled with
his image.

I was more drawn to the workshops because it was where
the people who were into the music were. I was quite moved

by what people said to me and what they wanted to know. This is my lifeblood, what I have been doing since I first realized what I was made of and who I was becoming. It is my need, my desire to live and grow as many branches of expression as I am able, to meet as many people who share the need to be met, and to send out a few warnings from time to time about what I see and feel us doing with this precious planet we live on. I take it upon myself to do that because that is who I am.

We are all connected. In South Africa and in New York. In Jerusalem and Cairo, in retirement homes and baby carriages, among the young and the not so young.

In Khayelitsha on the outskirts of Cape Town, my workshop took place in a large cement shed with simple appointments—a perfect venue for all of us who were there. This was a village that looked like a shantytown from the outside, but it was filled with wonderfully warm, beautifully kept homes. The people may not have had wealth, but they had a sense of family and togetherness that you could feel from everything and everyone.

I did an interview in their radio station, which was a trailer truck backed up to a building, and they told me with great depth of pride how they got their start during apartheid—how they had to rush out on the road to broadcast for twenty minutes before they had to take the rig down to avoid being hassled by government police.

They grew from that beginning into a regular radio station that played to all of South Africa. The sweat of their effort was still ingrained in their being and the gift of their forum was appreciated all the more.

I did not just fly in and fly out to do a gig. I was introduced to all the musicians in the town. I learned how black Mombasa music started at bus stops when the people entertained themselves in group singing and dancing competitions waiting for the buses to go home. To this day, there are competitions like that, which begin in many similar places after midnight—after the last buses of the day.

The folk music of South Africa is the real music of their lives. In the workshops there were hungry eyes and eager minds looking for a way to express themselves, their emotions, their thoughts, their beliefs. Their music comes naturally. We are all the same.

I told them I made lots of mistakes and a lot of great sounds when I was starting out. I told them I kept the great sounds and left the mistakes behind. Except for the ones that really were not mistakes at all. They were temporary blocks that became building blocks. That is music and that is life.

What they learned to do on the guitar in South Africa is rooted in their natural tendency to play xylophone-style, native instruments, some with only two strings. You can hear it in their rhythm patterns and in the wondrous sounds they make. We use what we have and we gain strength by building layers of new knowledge from that. We are all the same.

In South Carolina in the mid-1970s, I had my only racially tinged incident at a concert in more than thirty years. And it wasn't anything more than a hostile front being put on by a stage manager who knew his time of exclusion had come and gone. Less than a year later in southern Mississippi, an audience with Dixie flags and slogans from the Confederacy hanging from the rafters cheered every song and gave me and my band all the hospitality and warmth in their bones. It is not true that the sons have to be like their fathers. We are all the same and we are beginning for the first time in human history to begin to take that seriously.

I always wished I could really pick the guitar, to have the guitar sing the song. But my guitar is there to accompany my song. I am not Eric Clapton, who taught himself how to sing beautifully with his voice long after he was a master guitarist. He became a great singer. If you do something long enough with passion, you will do it well. My guitar does not sing my songs, but I hear my music in it. We can all grow and be all we were built to be. But we must admit to the changes that have happened to us. We must admit to the way we really feel. Today.

What we did as a generation in the 1960s was try to avoid being put in a box. We wanted no part of the labels that dismissed who we really were. We were individuals. American individuals.

The youth of today should understand that there is no such thing as Generation X. It is a label that was created by someone else. Just like the *hippie* label was created thirty years ago to lump too many free-thinking people under one umbrella to minimize their potential to question, to dare, to grow, to change.

It is important to find and read as much modern history as you can get your hands on. Know that no one is above the law in this nation and that we the people are not the only ones who can and must be held accountable for protecting or defiling freedom.

Militancy is not the way to change, any more than the obvious treason of too many politicians selling weapons to the enemy or sitting idly by while power brokers buy their votes to manipulate democracy for their own ends.

Nelson Mandela stood up for what was clearly right in South Africa, because he knew that his homeland and his people would die in their own dust if he did not. Martin Luther King, Jr., and Mahatma Gandhi acted in their time on their soils with the same convictions.

Our founders in America knew the same message and spelled it out clearly in the document we call the Constitution. Shouldn't we ask ourselves why the Congress and Senate work so hard to protect their positions, while they rarely act in good conscience for the good of the people who they are pledged to represent?

Is it our country's mission to make a farce of its democratic promise of freedom for all? Not while there are young voices and bright, independent minds to speak up and make waves. Not while there are singers and songwriters and novelists and poets and artists and free-thinking men and women who want it more.

Remember, racial division was overtly allowed by government to exist beyond the Emancipation Proclamation until the sixties, when equality had to be indelibly written into law. We are young in our task but never more poised to accomplish it. We have come too far to just follow the same sorry script. The songs we sing tell us so; we should listen to them more.

THE ZODIAC SONG

There is a secret that has been kept from man two
   thousand years;
And that secret is
that there are only twelve people on this Earth;
And those people have been symbolized by many symbols
they were called Twelve Tribes of Israel;

Twelve roads to the city . . . Twelve gates of Heaven
. . . Twelve inches in a foot;
Twelve months to the year . . . Twelve men on the jury,
Twelve days of Christmas . . . Twelve disciples of Jesus Christ.
Twelve manners of fruit on the tree good for the healing of
all nations, and these people are,

Aries . . . who is . . . I am . . . ain't I;
Taurus . . . who is . . . I have . . . don't I;
Gemini . . . who is . . . I think, I think,
I think so much, I wish I could stop thinking;
Cancer . . . who is . . . I feel, I feel
and there are no words that describe how I feel . . . ever;
Leo . . . who is . . . I will . . . or my will;

Virgo . . . who is . . . I analyze . . . I analyze;
Libra . . . who is . . . I balance, I balance,
I balance between those who know
and those who do not know;
Scorpio . . . who is . . . I desire, I desire,
I desire . . . I desire, I desire (ad infinitum)
Sagittarius,
Sagittarius . . . who is . . . I see, I see
. . . I see so much in what I'm doing
I cannot finish what I'm doing;
Capricorn . . . who is . . . I use, I use,
I use all of my experiences in order to Survive;
Aquarius . . . who is . . . I know,
I know . . . why do I know and no one around me
knows what I know;
Pisces . . . who is . . . I believe,
I believe . . . or there is nothing for me to believe in;

These are the twelve people who inherit the Earth;

. . . You are one of them and here are eleven others
and if you get to know the other eleven
. . . you will be able to get along
with everyone
all over the world.

I wrote that song from all of the comparative religions I
have read. They all make references to the zodiac as the first

science, which encompassed all other sciences we think of as separate today—physical, mental, and spiritual (or intuition)—before the word *spiritual* took its place, reinterpreted by the church itself.

We must write our history as we go forward and make sure it is handed down to the next generations. The youth must take it upon themselves to build upon the foundation and pick up the slack we leave them.

The myths are everywhere. All kids do not take drugs—in fact, a very small percentage of them do. Very small.

But kids do not forget what is done to them and by whom. We didn't. Yet, all kids wish for a happy life or a happy ending.

Our generation learned to live with each other as human beings, free to express what we thought and felt and came to know. We were the *first multinational American generation* . . . We believed what we were taught until we met each other face-to-face and found out it was not the truth.

No matter where our families came from, we were All-American kids. But if we were asked, could we name two things united about the United States of America? No shame. We are here to create them. This is the job of every generation born in this nation. And that is what every nation in the world must see for itself. We are all the same, human beings who have yet to tap into the full potential of what we have within us.

All I have to do to know the truth of this is to reflect on my earliest days in Bed-Stuy. I carry with me always the supreme joy of singing with friends on street corners, sharing songs and ideas with so many great musicians and poets and people of art and grace—in Greenwich Village and around the world. I understand the gift I have been given. It has always made me want to reach out and sing and write and experience the world with undying passion. I feel fortunate for having done so, stronger for continuing. And who among us does not realize that there is so much more to see and do and learn or communicate? Yes, we really are above the ground now and at the very least, we have learned that many of our voices can be heard through the noise *and* the silence.

Shalom, salaam aleichem

RICHIE HAVENS

In the cement shed at Khayelitsha. What an amazing experience.
(Photo by Kim Ludbrook, Cape Town Times)

acknowledgments

First, to my family, all of them:

My grandparents for their deep humanity and its effect on me, their first grandson. To my mother and father, Mildred and Richard, who worked day and night to keep us all safe. My brothers and sisters: Don, Beatrice, Alfred, Larry, Calvin, Michele, Lenny, and Gina. To all of my aunts and uncles, on both sides of the family, who peopled the world I grew up in. To Nancy Havens and my daughters: Nancy-2, Dhalia, Beka, and Rachel. My grandchildren: Nelson, Jessica, Mario, Amanda, and Chogal.

To those who helped me grow in Greenwich Village:

Len Chandler; Noel Stookey; Fred Neil; Vince Martin; Dino Valenti; Major Wiley; Bob Gibson and Bob (Hamilton) Camp; Dave Van Ronk; Jo Mapes; Casey Anderson; John Hammond, Jr.; Odetta; Tim Hardin; Carolyn Hester; Mary Travers; Peter Yarrow; Bob Dylan; Jimi Hendrix; Ram Jim and Paul Holder; Arnie Clapman; Shawn Phillips; Taj Mahal; Nina Simone; Tim Buckley; Carol Hunter; Jose Feliciano; John Sebastian; Lou Gos-

ACKNOWLEDGMENTS

sett, Jr.; Jerry Merrick; Josh White, Sr.; Josh White, Jr.; Bruce Murdoch; and all the others who had the incredible pleasure of being in the right place at the right time—because they wanted to be.

To the poets and artists who made me think and question:

Hugh (Wavy Gravy) Romney, Jack Kerouac, Allen Ginsberg, John Brent and Ram John Holder, Arnie Clapman, Siga Loggie, Salvador Dali, and those who gave guidance to my career through the early years: Manny Roth (Cafe Wha?), Howie Solomon (Cafe au Go Go), Joe Marra (Nite Owl Cafe), Rick Allmen (Cafe Bizarre), Jacob Solmon, Albert Grossman, John Court, and Clay Cole.

To the comedians in the Village:

Lenny Bruce, Ed Lauder, Richard Pryor, Bill Cosby, Rodney Dangerfield, Joan Rivers, The Ace Trucking Co., Jody Graber, Dick Gregory, Johnny Carson, and the other hundred and fifty or so who kept me in tears and sidesplitting laughter while we were all in the midst of changing times and the beginning of the real world.

To many other special friends I have known through the years:

Kenny Schneider, Dennis Persich, Paul Williams, Daniel Ben Zebulon, Emile Latimer, Joe Price, Ben Ryan, Herman Earnest, Darryle Johnson, Tony Broussard, David LeBolt, Willie Smith, David Noferi, Dennis the D, James (Booty) Neal, Louis

ACKNOWLEDGMENTS

Small, Keith Lambeth, Jack Scarrangella, Hui Cox, Pino Daniele, Ronny Sunshine, Roland Moussa, Greg Chansky, Richard Savage, David Russo, Marcia Wolfson, Patty Zarnowski, Johanan Vigoda, John Fisher, Mark Roth, Bernice Wise, Bea Hammerman, Stephanie Marco, Melanie, Paolo Soleri, Terry Urban, Joe Paniccioli, Tom Smith and Kevin Sanders of the War & Peace Foundation. And the Dalai Lama. . . . Someday it all will make sense.

To the members of the Natural Guard Children's Environmental Justice Organization:

All of whom contributed tirelessly to prove that children can and do change their communities for the better. And to the person who made it all work for them and for me: Diane Edmonds.

To Michael Sandlofer:

Whose idea for the North Wind Undersea Institute gave me the opportunity to find out firsthand that children were the only real environmentalists willing to make the changes we, as grown-ups, are still trying to make within ourselves.

Special thanks, of course, to my co-author, Steve Davidowitz:

A versatile, talented writer and true friend who gave up a full year of freelance assignments to help me put my experiences into this book. Thanks as well to James Earl Jones for his kind Foreword; to our editor, Tom Dupree; managing edi-

ACKNOWLEDGMENTS

tor, Robin Davis Gomez; and copy editor, Mark Hurst; to Steve's agent Flip Brophy and his brother Sid Davidowitz, who helped restore old photographs. To Europe-based Web site researcher Brian Mathieson, *Cape Town Times* reporter Willem Steenkamp and his photographer Kim Ludbrook, and all the other photographers whose pictures I have chosen: Leslie Hawes, Günter Zint, Evan Schneider, Milton Grand, Frank Fournier, Ernie (Joe) Paniccioli, Mauren Brodbeck, and Steve Davidowitz, too.

Thanks as well to the millions of friends that I have encountered along this way called Life. . . . This book is dedicated to all of you and to all the children in my life.

discography

STUDIO AND LIVE ALBUMS
Cuts to the Chase (Rhino, 1995)

> *Lives in the Balance*
> *They Dance Alone*
> *My Father's Shoes*
> *Darkness, Darkness*
> *The Hawk*
> *Young Boy*
> *The Times They Are a-Changin'*
> *Fade to Blue*
> *Intro/Old Love*
> *How the Nights Can Fly*
> *Comin' Back to Me*
> *Don't Pass It Up*
> *At a Glance*

Produced by Richie Havens.

Richie Havens, vocals, guitar; Jimmy Mack, bass; Billy Perry, guitar; Ed Barretini, drums; Greg Chansky, guitar; Louis Small, keyboards; Paul Chansky, keyboards; Chuck Mangione, flugelhorn.

Now (Solar, 1991)
>   *Angel*
>   *You Are the One*
>   *That's the Way I See You*
>   *After All These Years*
>   *Time After Time*
>   *Love Sometimes Says Goodbye*
>   *You're My Tomorrow*
>   *Let the Walls Fall Down*
>   *Message from the Doctor*
>   *It Ain't Over Till It's Over*

This album was later rereleased, against Richie's wishes, under the title *Yes,* with a title track added.

Richie Havens Live at the Cellar Door (Five-Star, 1990)
>   *Can't Make It Anymore*
>   *All Along the Watchtower*
>   *Helplessly Hoping*
>   *God Bless the Child*
>   *The Night They Drove Old Dixie Down*
>   *No More, No More*
>   *Preparation*
>   *Here Comes the Sun*
>   *Fire and Rain*
>   *Superman*
>   *Dolphins*
>   *Nobody Knows the Trouble I've Seen/My Sweet Lord*

Produced by Bernard Fox and Mark Roth.
Richie Havens, vocals, guitar; Paul Williams, guitar; Eric Oxendine, bass; Joe Price, percussion.

The first eight songs made up a live album recorded at the Cellar Door in 1970 by Bernard Fox but not released until 1990; the last four selections were produced by Mark Roth at Santa Monica Civic Auditorium in 1972.

Simple Things (RBI, 1987)

Drivin'
Simple Things
Songwriter
Passin' By
Wake Up and Dream
I Don't Wanna Know
Shouldn't We All Be Having a Good Time
Arrow Through Me
Runner in the Night

Produced by Jim Tullio.
Richie Havens, vocals, guitar; Bill Rupert, Ross Traut, Jim Tullio, Bruce Gaitsch, and Steve Burgh, guitars; Jim Hines, Wayne Stewart, Joe Pusateri, drums/percussion; Mark Colby, tenor sax; Steve Harman, harp; Ian Ward, Mark Ohlsen, Mike Halpin, Elmer Brown, Bill Dinwiddie, horns; Pat Leonard, Chris Cameron, C. J. Vanston, synthesizers; Lonnie Reaves, piano; Rusty Taylor, Tony Brown, bass; Robert Morgan, oboe; Michael Masters and an orchestral string section, strings; Josie Aiello, Diane

Holmes, Robin Robinson, Butch Stewart, and Brenda Mitchell, background vocals.

Richie Havens Sings Beatles and Dylan (Rykodisc, 1987)
>   *Here Comes the Sun*
>   *If Not for You*
>   *Lay Lady Lay*
>   *In My Life*
>   *Strawberry Fields Forever*
>   *All Along the Watchtower*
>   *Imagine*
>   *My Sweet Lord*
>   *It's All Over Now, Baby Blue*
>   *Eleanor Rigby*
>   *Just Like a Woman*
>   *The Long and Winding Road*
>   *Let It Be*
>   *License to Kill*
>   *The Times They Are a-Changin'*
>   *Working Class Hero*
>   *Rocky Raccoon*
>   *With a Little Help from My Friends*

Produced by Richie Havens and Douglas Yeager.
Richie Havens, vocals, guitar; Douglas Yeager, guitar; Paul Williams, guitar; Cliff Eberhardt, guitar; Carol Steele, percussion; Michael Raye, synth bass, drums.

This is a studio album and features rerecordings of some songs performed on other albums—with new arrangements.

Common Ground (Connexions, 1983)

Death at an Early Age
Gay Cavalier
Lay Ye Down Boys
This Is the Hour
Stand Up
Dear John
Leave Well Enough Alone
Moonlight Rain
Things Must Change

Produced by Pino Daniele and Richie Havens.
Richie Havens and Pino Daniele, vocals, guitar.

Recorded in Milan, featuring EMI studio musicians.

Connections (Elektra/Asylum, 1980)

Mama We're Gonna Dance
Every Night
You Send Me
We've Got Tonight
Ol' 55
Goin' Back to My Roots
Dreams
She Touched My Heart
Fire Down Below
Here's a Song

Produced by Denny Rendell.
Richie Havens, vocals, guitar; Jeff Baxter, David Spinozza, Elliot

Randell, and Rick Derringer, guitars; Michael Olatunji and co.—Allan Schwartzberg, Montego Joe, Andy Newmark, Steve Gadd—drums/percussion; Jack Waldman, Richard Tee, keyboards; David Woodford, tenor sax; David Lebolt, Doug Katsaros, synthesizers; Bob Babbitt and Chuck Rainey, bass; Gloria Agostini, harp; Lou Christie, Ann Lang, Clydie King, Linda November, and Gail Wynters, background vocals.

Mirage (A&M, 1977)
> *Live It Up (One Time)*
> *Shadows of the Past*
> *I Don't Complain*
> *Touch the Sky*
> *Billy John*
> *We All Wanna Boogie*
> *Avalon*
> *Aviation Man*
> *Nobody Left to Crown*
> *The End*

Produced by Christopher Bond.
Richie Havens, vocals, guitar; Darryle Johnson, lead and rhythm guitars; Tony Broussard, bass; Herman Ernest III, drums; Paul Williams, guitars; David LeBolt and William Smith, keyboards; Tom Scott, saxophone; Gary Coleman, percussion.

The End of the Beginning (A&M, 1976)

I'm Not in Love
We Can't Hide It Anymore
Dreaming as One
You Can Close Your Eyes
I Was Educated by Myself
Daughter of the Night
If Not for You
Do It Again
Wild Night
Long Train Running

Produced by David Kershenbaum.
Richie Havens, vocals, guitar; Booker T. Jones, organ; Herman Ernest, drums; William Smith and Joey Oliver, keyboards; Tony Broussard, bass; Darryle Johnson and Steve Cropper, guitars; Jeff Baxter, steel guitar.

Mixed Bag II (Polydor, 1974)

Ooh Child
Headkeeper
Wandering Angus
Sad Eyed Lady of the Lowlands
Someone Suite
Band on the Run
The Longer
The Makings of You
The Indian Prayer

Produced by Richie Havens.

Richie Havens, vocals, guitar; Bernard Purdie, drums; Eric Oxendine, Bob Siegler, and Greg Reeves, bass; Paul Williams, guitar; Ralph Shuckett, piano.

Portfolio (Polydor, 1973)

> *It Was a Very Good Year*
> *Dreaming My Life Away*
> *23 Days in September*
> *I Know I Won't Be There*
> *I Don't Need Nobody*
> *Woman*
> *What's Goin' On*
> *Tightrope*
> *Mama Loves You*

Produced by Richie Havens.

Richie Havens, vocals, guitar; Daniel Ben Zebulon, percussion; Eric Oxendine, bass; Eric Weissberg, Paul Williams, and Jerry Friedman, guitar.

Richie Havens on Stage (Polydor, 1972)

> *From the Prison*
> *Younger Men Grow Older*
> *God Bless the Child*
> *High Flying Bird*
> *Tupelo Honey*
> *Just Like a Woman*

Handsome Johnny
Where Have All the Flowers Gone
Rocky Raccoon
Teach the Children
Minstrel from Gault
Freedom

Produced by Richie Havens.
Richie Havens, vocals, guitar; Paul Williams, guitar; Emile Latimer, congas; Eric Oxendine, bass.

A live album recorded at BBC Television Centre, London; Santa Monica Civic Auditorium, California; The Cellar Door, Washington, D.C.; and Westbury Music Fair, New York.

"The Great Blind Degree" (Stormy Forest, 1971)
What About Me
Fire and Rain
See Me, Feel Me
In These Flames
Think About the Children
Fathers and Sons
Teach Your Children
What Have We Done

Produced by Richie Havens.
Richie Havens, vocals, guitar; Emile Latimer, percussion; Eric Oxendine, bass; Paul Williams, guitar; Bob Margoleff, synthesizer.

Alarm Clock (Stormy Forest, 1971)

 Here Comes the Sun
 To Give All Your Love Away
 Younger Men Grow Older
 Girls Don't Run Away
 End of the Seasons
 Some Will Wait
 Patient Lady
 Missing Train
 Alarm Clock

Produced by Richie Havens and Mark Roth.
Richie Havens, vocals, guitar; Bill LaVorgna, drums; Eric Oxen-dine, bass; Paul Williams, guitar; Daniel Ben Zebulon, congas; Alan Hand, piano.

Stonehenge (Stormy Forest, 1970)

 Open Our Eyes
 Minstrel from Gault
 It Could Be the First Day
 Ring Around the Moon
 It's All Over Now, Baby Blue
 There's a Hole in the Future
 I Started a Joke
 Prayer
 Tiny Little Blues
 Shouldn't All the World Be Dancing

Produced by Richie Havens and Mark Roth.
Richie Havens, vocals, guitar; Daniel Ben Zebulon, drums, con-

gas; Eric Oxendine, bass; Bill LaVorgna, drums; Paul Williams and Monte Dunn, guitars.

Richard P. Havens, 1983 (Verve, 1969)

Stop Pulling and Pushing Me
For Haven's Sake
Strawberry Fields Forever
What More Can I Say, John
I Pity the Poor Immigrant
Lady Madonna
Priests
Indian Rope Man
Cautiously
Just Above My Hobby Horse's Head
She's Leaving Home
Putting Out the Vibration, and Hoping It Comes Home
The Parable of Ramon
With a Little Help from My Friends
Wear Your Love Like Heaven
Run Shaker Life / Do You Feel Good

Produced by Richie Havens and Mark Roth.

Richie Havens, vocals, guitar; Arnie Moore, Carol Hunter, Brad Campbell, and Stephen Stills, bass; Skip Prokop and Don Mac-Donald, drums; Weldon Myrick, steel guitar; Paul Williams, guitar; Jeremy Steig, flute; Colin Walcott, sitar; Paul Harris, piano; Warren Bernhardt, keyboards; John Ord, piano, organ; Carter C. C. Collins, congas.

And the "P." stands for Pearce, same as Richie's father.

Something Else Again (Verve, 1968)

No Opportunity Necessary, No Experience Needed
Inside of Him
The Klan
Don't Listen to Me
Sugarplums
From the Prison
New City
Run Shaker Life
Maggie's Farm
Something Else Again

Produced by John Court.
Richie Havens, vocals, guitar; Warren Bernhardt, keyboards; Jeremy Steig, flute; Don MacDonald and Skip Prokop, drums; Eddie Gomez, Don Payne, and Denny Gerrard, bass; Paul Williams and Adrian Guillery, guitar.

Mixed Bag (Verve, 1967)

High Flyin' Bird
I Can't Make It Anymore
Morning, Morning
Adam
Follow
Three Day Eternity
Sandy
Handsome Johnny
San Francisco Bay Blues

Just Like a Woman
Eleanor Rigby

Produced by John Court.

Richie Havens, vocals, guitar; Paul Harris, keyboards; Harvey Brooks, bass; Bill LaVorgna, drums; Howard Collins and Paul Williams, guitar; Joe Price, tabla.

COMPILATIONS
Résumé: The best of Richie Havens, (Rhino, 1993)

High Flying Bird
Drown in My Own Tears
Morning, Morning
Just Like a Woman
Dolphins
Here Comes the Sun
God Bless the Child
The Klan
Handsome Johnny
Follow
Younger Men Grow Older
Medley: Run Shaker Life/Do You Feel Good
What About Me
Minstrel from Gault
Rocky Raccoon
San Francisco Bay Blues
Freedom

Compilation by Neil Portman and Bruce Pollock.

Collection (Rykodisc, 1987)

Woman

What's Going On

Younger Men Grow Older

What About Me

There's a Hole in the Future

Fire and Rain

It Could be the First Day

Minstrel from Gault

Tightrope

Open Our Eyes

Prayer

Missing Train

I Started a Joke

Teach Your Children

San Francisco Bay Blues

High Flying Bird

Here Comes the Sun

Richie Havens (Polydor, 1975)

Here Comes the Sun

Ooh Child

I Don't Need Nobody

What About Me

Minstrel from Gault

End of the Season

It Was a Very Good Year

Someone Suite

Open Our Eyes
She's Leaving Home
Tightrope
I Pity the Poor Immigrant
The Indian Prayer

Compilation by Bob Clifford.

A Richie Havens Record (1969)

I'm Gonna Make You Glad
It Hurts Me
Chain Gang
Drown in My Own Tears
I'm on My Way
Babe, I'm Leavin'
Nora's Dove
Daddy Roll 'Em
The Bag I'm In

UNAUTHORIZED ALBUMS (PULLED FROM CIRCULATION)
Electric Havens (1968)

Oxford Town
900 Miles from Home
I'm a Stranger Here
My Own Way
Boots of Spanish Leather
C. C. Rider
3:10 to Yuma
Shadow Town

RICHIE HAVENS ALSO APPEARS ON

Lifelines/Peter, Paul, and Mary (1995)

Earthrise: The Rainforest Album/Various Artists (1994)

Woodstock Diary/Various Artists (1994)

Can We Go Higher? A Song for the Victims of War/Various Artists (1992)

The Long Road/Cliff Eberhardt (1990)

Harry Chapin: The Tribute Album/Various Artists (1990) (Richie performs *WOLD*)

Please Don't Touch/Steve Hackett (1978)

Tommy/The London Symphony Orchestra (1972) (Richie performs *Eyesight to the Blind*)

American Children/Various Artists

When October Goes: Autumn Love Songs/Various Artists

MOTION PICTURE SOUNDTRACKS

The American Game

Boulevard of Broken Dreams (title song)

Brother Minister: The Assassination of Malcolm X

C. B.

Coming Home

Gumball Rally

Greased Lightning

Homer and Eddy

Matter of Struggle

Navy Seals

One Good Reason

Warriors of Virtue (title song: *Inside of You*)

Wired

Woodstock (Richie performs *Freedom*)

THEATER

Bohickee Creek

Electric God

Nexus

Peter and the Wolf (with the New York City Ballet at Town Hall)

RICHIE HAVENS'S SHORT LIST OF HIGHLY RECOMMENDED READING

The Prophet/Kahlil Gibran

Huna Self-Awareness/Dr. E. S. Nau

Crystal Skull/Alice Bryant and Phyllis Galde

The Biggest Con/Irwin A. Schiff

Book of the Hopi/Frank Waters

Steal This Book/Abbie Hoffman

Thinking Like a Mountain/John Seed, Joanna Macy, Pat Fleming, and Arnie NaESS

Dwight David Eisenhower's final speech as President of the United States, January 1960

ON THE WEB

Richie Havens: www.richiehavens.com

Richie's Web site includes his concert performance schedule for several months in advance. Additional information is available at: www.mathie.demon.co.uk

Jack Hammer: www.hammerhits.com

Jack's Web site is a trip. On it he says his grandmother was the first person to say, "Goodness gracious, great balls of fire."

a parting word
from steve davidowitz

The first time I saw Richie Havens was in the Gaslight Cafe in the early 1960s, and this is how powerful an impression he made on me: Instead of using the proceeds of a winning 37–1 long shot at Aqueduct to buy a car to run around Rutgers University, I bought my first guitar, even though I didn't play at the time.

Three decades later, I was covering the 1997 Belmont Stakes for an Internet magazine when Richie performed an impromptu version of "Here Comes the Sun" with trainer Bob Baffert at the press party two days before the big race. Baffert knew enough to keep his day job, and I knew enough to make sure I saw Richie play again in New York City a few weeks later.

What I saw and heard that summer night blew me away and reminded me of what Roger McGuinn (later of the Byrds) used to say about Richie during his Village years: "Richie was so good, you didn't want to go on after he performed. Either the audience would have given him all their money when he passed the hat, or they'd get up and follow him out the door to the next coffeehouse."

The Richie Havens who plays and tells stories today is even more compelling. It's been a privilege to help him share his incredible experiences, his art, his encounters with so many gifted people, and his intelligent perceptions about life in our rapidly changing world. Now that you have traveled along with Richie in this book, don't be surprised if you suddenly feel inspired to play the guitar, or sketch a portrait, or write a poem, or do all of that and more. It's happened before, to many people Richie has touched throughout the world—including me. That is Richie Havens's enduring legacy.

Steve Davidowitz can be reached at: davidwtz@warwick.net

index

A Day in the Garden, 278–89
A&M Records, 221–22
Ace, Johnny, 169
Alarm Clock (Havens), 159–62
"Alarm Clock" (Havens), lyrics to, 160–61
Alpert, Herb, 221
Amoros, Sandy, 7
Andersen, Eric, 38
Anderson, Casey, 39–40
ARM, 223–24

Bari, Italy, 227
Battle of the Record Labels, 227–29
Beatles, 136–37
Bedford-Stuyvesant, Brooklyn, 4–9
    changes in, 9–11
    "The Bells of Rhymney," 67–68
    lyrics to, 68–69
Berry, Chuck, 94
Big Brother and the Holding Company, 101
Big Brown, 54
Bloomfield, Mike, 104–5
Blues Project, 38, 108, 109–10
Blumenfeld, Roy, 109
Bohickee Creek (Unger), 84–85

Brady, Victor "Superman," 31–34
Brenner, David, 51
Brent, John, 35–36
Brownsville community, Brooklyn, 6–7
Bruce, Lenny, 51
Burr, Aaron, ghost of, 81
Butterfield, Paul, 104

Cafe Bizarre, 81
Cafe Wha?, 31–34
Camp, Bob, 35
Campanella, Roy, 7
Carson, Johnny, 114, 116
Catch My Soul (film), 85
"Cautiously" (Weinstock), lyrics to, 137–38
Cecil, Malcolm, 237–39
Chamberlain, Wilt "the Stilt," 102
Chandler, Len, 66
Cheetah, 101–2
Clapman, Arnold, 222–24
Clapton, Eric, 296
Close Encounters of the Third Kind (film), 250–52
coffeehouses, 74
Cohen, Myron, 51

INDEX

Common Ground (Havens and Daniele), 225–27, 229
Connections (Havens), 224
Cooke, Sam, 82, 170
Cosby, Bill, 50
Court, John, 110–11, 117
Crosby, Stills, & Nash, 277
Curb, Mike, 217–19
Cuts to the Chase (Havens), 234

Dangerfield, Rodney, 50
Daniele, Pino, 225–27
DePass, Steve, 147
Doggett, Bill, 19
Doggett, Claude, 18–19
Domenici, Pete, 198–99
Donovan, 283, 289
Dylan, Bob, 43, 95, 137, 141–42, 143–45
  meeting, 76–77

"Earth, Moon and Stars," lyrics to, 209
Edmonds, Diane, 197
Electric God (Hammer), 204–6
Elektra-Asylum, 224
Elliot, Cass, 42
ELO Productions, 231
The End of the Beginning (Havens), 221–22
"End of the Seasons" (Havens), 161–62
  lyrics to, 162–63
Explorer's Club, 189

Fisher, John, 164–65, 167, 172
Flamingos, 82
Flanders, Tommy, 110
Frankie Lymon and the Teenagers, 14
"Freedom" (Havens), 126–29
  lyrics to, 127
The Freedom Ship, 193

Fugs, 141
Fuqua, Harvey, 82

Gaslight, 38
Gate of Horn, 78
Gay, Beatrice Elizabeth, 6–7
Gerry, Alan, 279–81, 285–86
Ghandi, Mahatma, 297
Gibson, Bob, 35
Gore, Al, 198–99
Gossett, Lou, Jr., 111–13
Graber, Jody, 51–53
Greased Lightning (film), 85
The Great Blind Degree (Havens), 210–11
Green, Gary, 168
Greenwich Village, 26–30
  coffeehouses, 74
  comedic talents in, 50–53
  musical talents in, 31–49
  Washington Square Park, 53–55
Griffey, Dick, 231
Grossman, Albert, 35, 78–80, 95, 151–53, 154
Grundman, Roni, 243–50
Gunn, Moses, 84

Hammer, Jack, 202–6, 235–38
"Handsome Johnny" (Gossett and Havens), 113–17
  lyrics to, 114–17
Hardin, Tim, 36–38, 108, 109, 121
Harrison, George, 163
Harts Island jail, 56
Havens, Alfred, 184
Havens, Donald, 188
Havens, Leonard, 184–85
Hayden, Maury. See Weinstock, Lotus
Hendrix, Jimi, 101–6
Henske, Judy, 43–44
"Here Comes the Sun" (Harrison), 163

Hester, Carolyn, 41
Hostage (Havens), 233

Ian, Janis, 108, 109
Infante, David, 204–5
Irose, Chuck, 74

Jackson, Michael, 293
Jerusalem, visit to, 240–52
Jimi James and the Blue Flame,
    103
Jones, James Earl, 84
    foreword by, ix–xii
Joplin, Janis, 101

Kalb, Danny, 38, 109
Katz, Steve, 110
Kauffman, Jeffrey, 212
Keys, Clarence "Eighty-Eight," 17
Khayelitsha, Cape Town, South
    Africa, 294–95
King, Martin Luther, Jr., 297
Kooper, Al, 109, 110
Kulberg, Andy, 109

Lang, Michael, 2
Lauder, Ed, 50
LaVorgna, Bill, 157
Lennon, John, 166–69, 170, 172
Les Variations, 237
"Let's Lay Down Our Drum"
    (Murdoch), lyrics to, 90–91
Little Carnegie Hall, 92
Lovin' Spoonful, 42

McCartney, Paul, 166–68
McCloud, Daniel Alexander. See
    Natoga
McKay, Tony, 54
McPhatter, Clyde, 82
*The Magic Garden of Stanley
    Sweetheart* (film), 218
Mandela, Nelson, 297

Marcellus, 41
Marco, Stephanie, 253–57
Margoleff, Bob, 162
Marin, Cheech, 223
Marra, Joe, 37
Marx, David, 291
Meader, Vaughn, 50
Melanie, 283, 289
MGM, 151, 156
    sale of, 215–20
Michaels, Gene, 74–75
Middle East, travel to, 239
Minnelli, Liza, 99
Mirage (Havens), 222
Mitchell, John, 43
Mitchell, Joni, 289
Mixed Bag (Havens), 111, 118, 234
Mixed Bag II (Havens), 219–20
"Moonlight Rain" (Havens and
    Daniele), 225–26
    lyrics to, 226–27
Morrison, Jim, 101
Moss, Jerry, 221
Moussa, Roland, 219
Mugwumps, 42
Murdoch, Bruce, 87–90, 139
Music of My Mind (Wonder), 162

Nathan, Abbie, 241–43
Natoga, 2, 80–81
Natural Guard, 197–99
Neil, Fred, 31, 45–49, 66
New York University, 53
Newcombe, Don, 7
Newport Folk Festival, 85
Night Owl, 36–37
North Wind Undersea Institute,
    187–97
Now (Havens), 231

Ochs, Phil, 38
Odetta, 39

O'Gara, Laurie, 191
On Location Systems, 232–33

Parker, Tom, Colonel, 98
Paxton, Tom, 38
Pendergrass, Teddy, 82
Perfect Harmony (film), 85
Perkins, Carl, 94
Perry, Billy, 234
Peter, Paul, and Mary, 35
Phillips, Sam, 98
Polydor, 219
PolyGram, 219–20
"Prayer" (Havens), lyrics to, 158–59
Presley, Elvis, 97–100, 170
Pryor, Richard, 50, 171

Ray, Johnnie, 40–41
Redding, Otis, 170
Résumé: The Best of Richie Havens (Havens), 234
Rhino Records, 234
Richard P. Havens, 1983 (Havens), 156–57
Richie Havens on Stage (Havens), 217
Rio de Janeiro, annual song and performance competition in, 213–14
Rivers, Joan, 50
Robinson, Jackie, 7
Robinson, Smokey, 59–60
Romney, Hugh, 35
Roth, Manny, 31
Roth, Mark, 153, 165–66
Rush, Tom, 38
Rykodisc, 229–31

Sadat, Anwar, 235–36
Sahl, Mort, 51
Sainte-Marie, Buffy, 38–39
Salvation Club, 166

Sandlofer, Michael, 173–83, 186–97
Savage, Richard, 232
Schneider, Kenny, 16, 19–21, 24–25, 41, 264
Schoenbaum, Jerry, 108–10, 219
Scott, Bobby, 212
Sebastian, John, 42
Seeger, Pete, 38
"Shalom, Salaam Aleichem" (Havens), 237–39, 240
  lyrics to, 240
Simone, Nina, 146–50
Simple Things (Havens), 231
Sinatra, Frank, 161
Sly and the Family Stone, 277
Socoloff, Danny, 281–83
Solmon, Jacob (Jack), 82–92
Something Else Again (Havens), 117
Soul Stirrers, 82
South Africa, visit to, 292–95
Steinberg, David, 51
Stonehenge (Havens), 157–59
Stookey, Noel, 31, 35
Stormy Forest Records, 154
Supac, Darrell, 284

Taganasi, Ron, 215
Tanners, 74
"Think About the Children" (Scott), 212
  lyrics to, 212–13
The Tonight Show, 113–14, 116
Tork, Peter, 83
Townshend, Peter, 277, 289
Travers, Mary, 35

Unger, Robert, 84

Valenti, Dino, 31, 41, 44–46, 267–68
Valenti, Marcellus, 267–68
Van Cleef, Ron, 215

INDEX

Van Ronk, Dave, 36, 38, 77
Velores, 82
Verve Folkways, 108–9
Vietnam War, 112–13
Vigoda, Johanan, 105, 153,
   154–56, 209, 231

Washington Square Park, 53–55
Wein, George, 89
Weinstock, Lotus, 41–42, 137
"What More Can I Say John?"
   (Havens), lyrics to, 139–40
White, Josh, 70
White, Josh, Jr., 70
Who, 277
"Who Am I," lyrics to, 208
Wiley, Major, 40–41
Williams, Keith, 82
Williams, Paul "Deano," 2, 80–82

Willis, Chuck, 169
Wolfson, Marcia, 222–24
Wonder, Stevie, 162
Woodstock, 1–3, 118–33, 274–79
   future festivals, 290
   twentieth anniversary festival,
     286–87
   twenty-fifth anniversary festival,
     286
   twenty-ninth anniversary
     festival, 278–89

Yanofsky, Zal, 42
Yarrow, Peter, 35, 172
Yes (Havens), 231

Zebulon, Daniel Ben. See Natoga
"The Zodiac Song" (Havens), 300
   lyrics to, 298–99